THE MICHELIN FIELD GUIDE TO

INSECTS

Note: Every effort has been made to ensure that the information contained in this Michelin Field Guide is as accurate and up-to-date as possible at the time of going to press. The authors, editors, consultants, and publishers of this book can not be held liable for any errors or omissions, nor for any consequences of using *The Michelin Field Guide to Insects*.

ISBN 1 85671 185 4

Michelin Tyre Public Limited Company
Edward Hyde Building, 38 Clarendon Road, Watford, Herts
WD1 1SX

A CIP record for this title is available from the British Library.

Edited by Neil Curtis. Designed by Richard Garratt.

The Publisher gratefully acknowledges the contribution of Premaphotos Wildlife who provided all the photographs in this Michelin Field Guide. Text by Ken Preston-Mafham.

Colour reproduction by Anglia Colour Ltd.

Printed in Spain by Graficromo SA.

INTRODUCTION

Insects are not difficult to find. From spring to autumn, wherever you go, whether it be in leafy woodland, rugged cliff-top, thyme-scented southern downland, or nettle-choked riverbank, you are sure to encounter a wealth of insects. In fact, you do not even have to leave home. Even the most carefully manicured of gardens, including those in the very centres of major cities, will have their quota of butterflies, flies, beetles, bugs, bees, and other six-legged denizens.

Most insects are rather small, so you will often need to get a good close look at your subject to be sure of making a reasonably accurate identification. For example, you would probably need to inspect the antennae to distinguish between a genuine bumble-bee and several kinds of flies which are so like bumble-bees that only the most experienced observer can spot the difference at a glance. Therefore, a cheap, folding hand-lens will probably be a good buy if you intend to spend much time looking at insects. A lens will also enable you to appreciate the beauty of many of our insects, much of which is often obscured simply because our eyes cannot focus closely enough.

IN THIS I-SPY GUIDE

There are over 20,000 different species of insects in the British Isles. Of these, 250 are included in this book. Although this might seem to be only a very small selection, the species illustrated have been carefully chosen to include many of the insects that you are most likely to notice and want to identify. Most of the really small and drab insects have been omitted, therefore, as have most rarities, or insects that are active only at night. There is also a large number of rather small and uninteresting insects that can be identified only with great difficulty by a specialist, and these, too, have been omitted. Some insects, which are not particularly common, but which are nevertheless quite abundant and widespread in certain habitats, have been included to stimulate your interest. A good example is the Dune Snail Bee, *Osmia aurulenta*, which can be quite common in the sandy seaside areas where many people take their holidays. This delightful little bee would be worth seeking out because of its fascinating nesting habits.

The following information is provided for each species where relevant:

- the Common Name in English by which the insect is best known, e.g., Red Admiral Butterfly. Many insects do not have individual common names, in which case the name of the group is given, e.g., Hover-fly.
- the Scientific Name (words usually derived from Latin or Greek) which includes the genus to which it belongs, e.g., *Vanessa*, and a species name, e.g. *atalanta*; thus the Red Admiral is *Vanessa atalanta*.
- the name of the insect family to which the species belongs, e.g., Nymphalidae for the Red Admiral Butterfly.
- the overall appearance of the insect. As far as possible non-technical terms are used but, on occasion, it is impossible to avoid these, especially where certain parts of the body are being described, e.g., pronotum (the upper surface of the first thoracic segment) or femur (the third segment of the insect leg, usually the largest part). If in doubt, refer to the line drawing, in which all the body parts are arrowed for easy reference.
- the length of the insect, or in some kinds, such as butterflies and moths, the wing span.
- the season when you are most likely to find the insect in an active state. Remember that in the south of the British Isles many insects will be on the move a week or two earlier than in the far north.
- where it is found, i.e., a brief description of the kinds of habitat most frequented by the insect, and its geographical distribution.
- insect facts, relating to information not included in the other sections, often concerning behaviour or the immature stages. Not every species included has this entry.

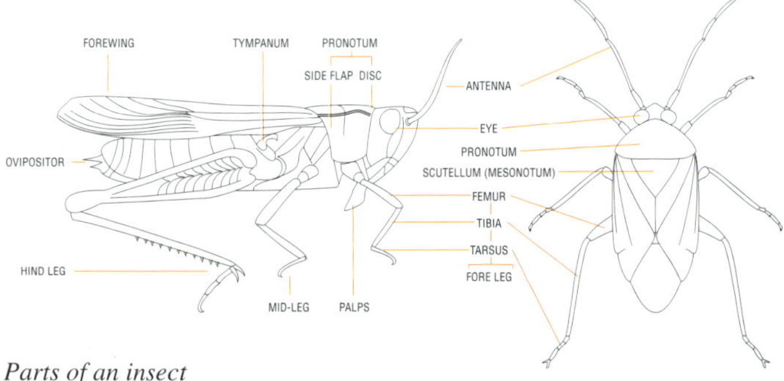

Parts of an insect

Greendrake

Scientific name: *Ephemera danica*
Family: Ephemeridae

Appearance: This is one of our larger mayflies, differing from most other mayflies in having dark cloudy spots on the wings. Other species of *Ephemera* have similar spots, but *E. danica* has a characteristic cream or off-white top to the abdomen, which is also distinguished by dark flecks. Mayflies can be distinguished from other insects by the following points in combination: wings held above the body when at rest; very short antennae; very long front legs, which are usually held up above the substrate (*see* plate); and two or three long, thread-like cerci or 'tails'.

Length: 15 mm (excluding the 'tails').

Season: April–September, commonest May–June.

Where is it found? Beside lakes and rivers over most of Britain.

Insect facts: Mayfly larvae (known as 'nymphs') live in fresh water. Mayflies are the only insects which moult when adult. The rather dull and hairy sub-imago (known as a 'dun') which emerges from the nymph soon sheds its skin to become the shinier adult or imago, known as a 'spinner'.

White-legged Damselfly

Scientific name: *Platycnemis pennipes*
Family: Platycnemididae

Appearance: The rather broad and flattened black-and-white legs of this damselfly easily distinguish it from other similar-looking kinds. The male (pictured) is a very pale whitish blue, while the female is often pure white, although she can also be pale green. Both sexes bear numerous narrow black markings.

Length: 35–40 mm.

Season: June–September.

Where is it found? By slow-moving rivers and small streams in lowland areas. In some areas, such as the Severn Vale in Gloucestershire and Worcestershire, this is a very common damselfly, but it is generally rather local and restricted to southern areas.

Insect facts: During courtship, the male hovers near the female and dangles his white legs in front of her face.

Large Red Damselfly

Scientific name: *Pyrrhosoma nymphula*
Family: Coenagriidae

Appearance: The male (illustrated) has a mostly pure-red abdomen, marked with bronzy black only towards its tip. In the female there is a bronzy black line all along the top of the abdomen. Both sexes have black legs, making it easy to distinguish this common species from the much rarer Small Red Damselfly (*Ceriagrion tenellum*) which has red legs.
Length: 35–40 mm.
Season: April–September, always the earliest species to appear.
Where is it found? In all types of fresh water, from tiny garden ponds and peaty pools on heathland to huge lakes, and in streams. Common in most of mainland Britain.
Insect facts: How do you distinguish a dragonfly from a damselfly? When at rest most damselflies hold their wings folded above their backs; dragonflies hold them out stiffly to the sides. Damselflies are also much slimmer bodied than dragonflies.

Blue-tailed Damselfly

Scientific name: *Ischnura elegans*
Family: Coenagriidae

Appearance: In the male there is always a blue ring near the tip of the abdomen. In the female (illustrated) this ring can be blue, lilac, or brown, while the sides of the thorax show the same range of colours (but blue only in the males). Two spots on either side of the head match the colour of the abdomen.
Length: 25–35 mm.
Season: March–October.
Where is it found? Common in any kind of freshwater habitat over most of the British Isles.
Insect facts: Females of the Blue-tailed Damselfly go about solo egg-laying, skulking among the water plants in which they lay their eggs.

Common Blue Damselfly

Scientific name: *Enallagma cyathigerum*
Family: Coenagriidae

Appearance: The males (illustrated) are blue and black, the females greenish grey and black. The male can easily be distinguished from the only other abundant blue damselfly, the Azure Damselfly (*see* next plate) by the two complete blue rings at the tip of the abdomen. In the Azure Damselfly the ring nearest the tip of the abdomen is partly black. The females are more difficult to distinguish but, in the Common Blue Damselfly, a spine projects downwards from the rear end.

Length: 30–35 mm.
Season: May–October.
Where is it found? Over most of the British Isles, in every kind of fresh water. Often abundant in garden ponds.
Insect facts: Damselflies eat other small insects, especially mosquitoes, tearing them apart with their surprisingly powerful jaws and dropping the indigestible bits such as legs and wings.

Azure Damselfly

Scientific name: *Coenagrion puella*
Family: Coenagriidae

Appearance: Note how the black markings of the male (left) encroach on to the rearmost of the two blue rings near the tip of the abdomen. This easily distinguishes this species from the Common Blue Damselfly. The female (right) often lacks the blue seen in the illustration. Several other similar species of *Coenagrion* occur in Britain, but all are very much rarer and seldom encountered.

Length: 30–35 mm.

Season: April–September.

Where is it found? Prefers muddy lakes and ponds with plenty of floating vegetation. Often occurs in huge numbers in the south, but absent from large areas of the north and from Ireland.

Insect facts: The damselflies illustrated are laying eggs in water plants. The male remains in tandem with his mate, using special claspers at the tip of his abdomen to grasp the top of her thorax, just behind the head.

Emerald Damselfly

Scientific name: *Lestes sponsa*
Family: Lestidae

Appearance: Both sexes are a deep shiny green, but the male (illustrated) eventually develops patches of bright powder-blue along the sides of the thorax, while the blue of his eyes also becomes more conspicuous with age (the females have bronzy brown eyes). Members of this family typically hold their wings out at an angle to their sides.
Length: 25–35 mm.
Season: June–October.
Where is it found? Found on still and slow-moving water throughout the British Isles, but always rather scattered.
Insect facts: The female of this species often submerges to lay her eggs in water plants, held in tandem by the male above her.

Beautiful Demoiselle

Scientific name: *Calopteryx virgo*
Family: Calopterygidae

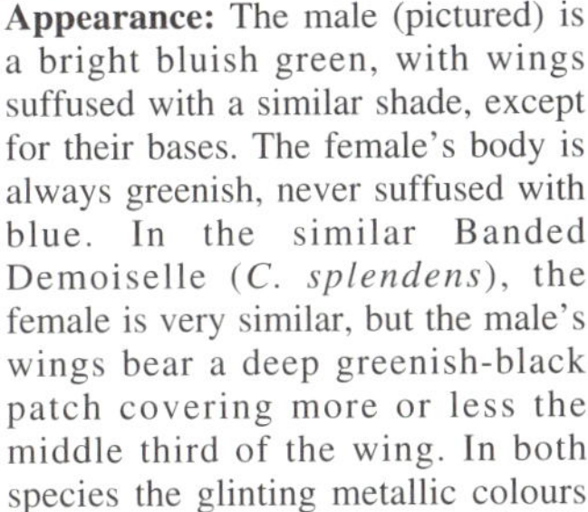

Appearance: The male (pictured) is a bright bluish green, with wings suffused with a similar shade, except for their bases. The female's body is always greenish, never suffused with blue. In the similar Banded Demoiselle (*C. splendens*), the female is very similar, but the male's wings bear a deep greenish-black patch covering more or less the middle third of the wing. In both species the glinting metallic colours make a most impressive spectacle when the insect flies in direct sunlight.
Length: 45 mm.
Season: April–September.
Where is it found? Breeds only in fast-flowing streams with sandy or gravelly bottoms. By contrast, the Banded Demoiselle prefers slow-flowing rivers with muddy bottoms. Both species are much commoner in the south.
Insect facts: The male Beautiful Demoiselle stands guard while his mate lays her eggs in emergent water plants.

Gold-ringed Dragonfly

Scientific name: *Cordulegaster boltonii*
Family: Cordulegasteridae

Appearance; With its large size and bold pattern of black and yellow rings, this can be mistaken for no other British dragonfly. Unlike in our other dragonflies, the compound eyes just about touch at the top of the head, rather than being so bulbous that they meet along quite an extended line. The male and female look very similar.

Length: 75–90 mm.
Season: May–September.
Where is it found? Widespread but local throughout mainland Britain, mostly on fast-flowing moorland streams.

Emperor Dragonfly

Scientific name: *Anax imperator*
Family: Aeshnidae

Appearance: The male (pictured) is the only large bright-blue dragonfly to be found in central and southern England. The apple-green female is equally unmistakable. In both sexes the thorax is greenish, and there is a black stripe down the centre of the abdomen. The male spends a lot of time patrolling his 'beat' over a pond, often until almost nightfall.
Length: 70–85 mm.
Season: May–October.
Where is it found? The Emperor Dragonfly prefers weedy lakes and ponds. It is restricted to central and southern areas.
Insect facts: The green females are well camouflaged as they lay their eggs inside floating water plants, avoiding the troublesome males patrolling overhead and the sharp eyes of birds, such as the hobby, which preys mainly on large dragonflies.

Brown Hawker Dragonfly

Scientific name: *Aeshna grandis*
Family: Aeshnidae

Appearance: This is the only large brown dragonfly which is at all likely to be seen in the British Isles. The blue spots on the abdomen are found only in the male but, otherwise, the sexes are difficult to distinguish in the field. The amber wings and blue eyes distinguish it from the rare Norfolk Hawker (*A. isosceles*) which has clear wings and greenish eyes.
Length: 65–75 mm.
Season: June–October.
Where is it found? In lakes and large ponds, especially gravel pits. Common in south-eastern and central England, rare in the west and north and in Ireland; not found in Scotland.
Insect facts: Dragonfly nymphs live in water. The nymph's most remarkable feature is a 'mask' which it shoots out to grasp prey, before pulling the victim back to be eaten. The mature nymph leaves the water and climbs a plant stem, and then the adult emerges through a split in the nymph's back.

Southern Hawker Dragonfly

Scientific name: *Aeshna cyanea*
Family: Aeshnidae

Appearance: The male (pictured) is mostly brown and green, with blue occurring only on the rearmost third of the abdomen and at its base; eyes blue. The female is similar but lacks the blue, and the eyes are greenish yellow. Both sexes bear broad green stripes (almost blobs) on top of the thorax. In the male Common Hawker (*A. juncea*) the stripes are narrow, while the blue marks occur throughout the abdomen; the female is brown and yellow and has no stripes on top of the thorax.

Length: 70–80 mm.
Season: June–October, sometimes into November.
Where is it found? On lowland lakes and ponds, mainly in southern and central areas, and absent from Ireland and Scotland. Often found a long way from water in woodland rides and along hedges.
Insect facts: The female Southern Hawker lays her eggs in old stumps and rotten tree roots above the water-line. When the winter rains come and water-levels rise the eggs hatch.

Migrant Hawker Dragonfly

Scientific name: *Aeshna mixta*
Family: Aeshnidae

Appearance: With its blue, brown, and black colour pattern, the male (pictured) is similar to the male of the Common Hawker. In the Migrant Hawker, however, there are only two small yellowish spots on top of the thorax. The females of the two species are very similar, but the Migrant Hawker is smaller.
Length: 60–70 mm.
Season: August–October.
Where is it found? In lakes and ponds, tending to avoid the acid moorland and heathland pools preferred by the Common Hawker. A southern species, absent from Scotland and Ireland.
Insect facts: The Migrant Hawker gets its name from its habit of migrating long distances, often in huge swarms.

Keeled Skimmer Dragonfly

Scientific name: *Orthetrum coerulescens*
Family: Libellulidae

Appearance: The male is blue, the female brown; the wing bases are clear in both sexes and there are usually two pale stripes on top of the thorax. The Keeled Skimmer is smaller and more slender than the Black-tailed Skimmer (*O. cancellatum*) which prefers gravel pits and lakes with muddy bottoms, and has a black-tipped abdomen and no thoracic stripes.
Length: 40–50 mm.
Season: May–August.
Where is it found? The Keeled Skimmer is restricted to the southern parts of the British Isles, in bog pools on heaths and moors.
Insect facts: Males of the skimmers and chasers are yellowish brown when they first emerge, and thereby resemble the females. The blue colour gradually appears as the males age. When mating, dragonflies adopt the so-called 'wheel' posture, as illustrated.

Four-spotted Chaser Dragonfly

Scientific name: *Libellula quadrimaculata*
Family: Libellulidae

Appearance: The body is more tapered than in any other British dragonfly, while the amber wing bases are unique. There are usually some blackish smudges towards the wing-tips. Males and females are almost identical, with yellowish-brown bodies, as the male never turns blue.
Length: 40–45 mm.
Season: April–September, commonest June–July.
Where is it found? Most often in boggy ponds on heaths and moors, but also sometimes very common on gravel pits. Scattered throughout the British Isles.
Insect facts: Four-spotted Chasers mate on the wing, taking just a few seconds. The male then hovers nearby while the female dips her tail in the water and washes off her eggs.

Broad-bodied Chaser Dragonfly

Scientific name: *Libellula depressa*
Family: Libellulidae

Appearance: This is by far the stockiest of our dragonflies, with a short and relatively broad abdomen. The male (illustrated) is blue, while the female is brown, and both sexes have large yellow spots along the sides of the abdomen. The black wing bases easily separate it from either of the skimmers, while the yellow spots are absent in the much rarer Scarce Chaser (*Libellula fulva*).
Length: 40–45 mm.

Season: April–September, commonest June–July.
Where is it found? On all types of still waters, often in garden ponds, mostly in the south, and absent from Scotland and Ireland.
Insect facts: In most skimmers, chasers, and darters the males hunt from a favoured perch, returning over and over again to the same place after each foray.

Common Darter Dragonfly

Scientific name: *Sympetrum striolatum*
Family: Libellulidae

Appearance: The male (illustrated) is rather a dull brick red, while the females are brown. The abdomen is not noticeably thickened towards the tip, and near the rear of each segment there is a pair of small black dots, ringed with yellow. The black legs are marked with longitudinal pale-yellowish stripes.
Length: 30–40 mm.
Season: July–October, sometimes out in June, and often lasting well into November.
Where is it found? On all types of still waters and on slow-moving rivers, almost throughout the British Isles, but commonest towards the south.
Insect facts: Common Darters lay eggs in tandem. The male grasps the back of the female's head with the claspers at the tip of his abdomen, and the pair dips up and down to wash off the eggs.

Ruddy Darter Dragonfly

Scientific name: *Sympetrum sanguineum*
Family: Libellulidae

Appearance: The much more brilliant red of the male Ruddy Darter (illustrated), is usually sufficient to separate it from the male Common Darter. The abdomen of the male Ruddy Darter is also thickened towards the end, making it rather club shaped, and there are no pairs of yellow-ringed black spots, as found in the Common Darter. The female is yellowish brown, and the legs are entirely black in both sexes.
Length: 30–40 mm.
Season: July–October.
Where is it found? On ponds, lakes, and slow-flowing streams, rather local and mainly in the south.
Insect facts: Ruddy Darters also lay their eggs in tandem, but tend to brush the eggs off on to plants growing in shallow water, rather than dipping into open water.

Black Darter Dragonfly

Scientific name: *Sympetrum scoticum*
Family: Libellulidae

Appearance: The Black Darter is the smallest British dragonfly, and also the latest to appear on the wing. Newly emerged males are brownish yellow, like the females, but gradually become suffused with black as they get older.

Length: 25–30 mm.
Season: August–October, sometimes into November.
Where is it found? The Black Darter is almost restricted to peaty pools on heaths and moors, throughout the British Isles.
Insect facts: Dragonflies catch their prey on the wing in a 'basket' formed by their spiny legs.

Mottled Grasshopper

Scientific name: *Myrmeloetettix maculatus*
Family: Acrididae

Appearance: Its small size makes the Mottled Grasshopper fairly easy to distinguish from several other similar-looking common grasshoppers. Also look for the slight thickening towards the tips of the antennae, this feature being more prominent in the male (illustrated) than in the female. The pattern is very variable, and so is the colour. The sides of the pronotum (behind the head) are very sharply angled inwards, with two conspicuous V-shaped marks. The rather similar (and much rarer) Rufous Grasshopper (*Gomphocerippus rufus*) has white tips to the antennae, and lives mainly on chalk and limestone downlands.
Length: 10–20 mm.
Season: June–October.
Where is it found? On heaths, moors, downland, and other dry bare places, throughout the British Isles.
Insect facts: The song of the Mottled Grasshopper is a series of short, rapidly repeated chirps, starting fairly softly and gradually increasing in intensity.

Common Field Grasshopper

Scientific name: *Chorthippus brunneus*
Family: Acrididae

Appearance: The commonest colour is brown, but you may also find green, black, or grey specimens. The most beautiful variation is the pink form illustrated. The sides of the pronotum (behind the head) are sharply angled inwards, but not to the extent seen in the Mottled Grasshopper. The underside of the Common Field Grasshopper is conspicuously hairy, and the wings extend well beyond the tip of the body in the male, and just beyond the tip in the female (illustrated). The tip of the abdomen is usually reddish, especially in the male.
Length: Male 15–19 mm; female 19–25 mm.
Season: June–November.
Where is it found? On dry grassland of all kinds, throughout the British Isles. It is often common on garden lawns.
Insect facts: The song is a series of brief chirps.

Meadow Grasshopper

Scientific name: *Chorthippus parallelus*
Family: Acrididae

Appearance: Both sexes are almost always a rather shiny green. In the female (illustrated) the forewings are very short, which easily distinguishes her from all our other similar-looking grasshoppers. The male's forewings stop well short of the tip of the abdomen. The hindwings in both sexes are tiny, making flight impossible. The side ridges of the pronotum (behind the head) are only very slightly incurved.
Length: Male 10–15 mm; female 15–22 mm.
Season: July–October.
Where is it found? In any type of grassland, throughout Britain, but much commoner in the south, and absent from Ireland.
Insect facts: Grasshoppers produce their 'songs' by a method called stridulation. By moving the back legs up and down, a series of pegs on their inner sides rubs against special enlarged veins on the forewings, producing a buzz or chirp.

Common Green Grasshopper

Scientific name: *Omocestus viridulus*
Family: Acrididae

Appearance: The females are usually green, but can have brown or pinkish sides, although even then the top is still green. Males are usually green, but occasionally brown, with just a little green on the head and pronotum. In the female (illustrated) the wings always fail to reach the tip of the body. In the male they just protrude beyond the tip of the abdomen, but not to the extent seen in the Common Field Grasshopper, in which the reddish abdomen-tip is never seen.

Length: Male 14–18 mm; female 17–21 mm.
Season: June–October.
Where is it found? In grass, throughout the British Isles.
Insect facts: The male's song consists of a ticking sound, starting rather softly and gradually building up, then falling away, and finally ending abruptly.

Speckled Bush-cricket

Scientific name: *Leptophyes punctatissima*
Family: Tettigoniidae

Appearance: This green bush-cricket is sprinkled with tiny dark-brown dots. There is a broad brown stripe down the middle of the male's back (on left), but in the female (on right) the stripe is narrower and more yellowish. The female's forewings are reduced to tiny flaps, but these are larger and saddle-like in the male. Neither sex has hindwings, so they cannot fly. The female's short, broad ovipositor curves upwards from the rear of her abdomen.
Length: 10–18 mm.
Season: July–November.
Where is it found? In nettle beds, bramble patches, at the base of roadside hedges, and in woodland rides. It is common in southern and central areas, but rare in the north, and absent from Scotland.
Insect facts: The Speckled Bush-cricket eats mainly leaves, especially brambles, but also eats small insects.

Oak Bush-cricket

Scientific name: *Meconema thalassinum*
Family: Tettigoniidae

Appearance: This is the bush-cricket most likely to be found inside houses, as both sexes are fully winged, and are attracted to lights. This insect is usually a very pale green – quite unlike any other bush-crickets – with a yellowish stripe down the centre of the back. The male (illustrated) has very long, curved claspers at the tip of his abdomen, while the female's ovipositor projects well beyond the ends of the wings.

Length: 13–17 mm.
Season: July–November.
Where is it found? In woodlands, gardens, and orchards.
Insect facts: Bush-crickets and grasshoppers can be distinguished at a glance. Bush-crickets have very long thread-like antennae, while in grasshoppers the antennae are much shorter and stouter.

Great Green Bush-cricket

Scientific name: *Tettigonia viridissima*
Family: Tettigoniidae

Appearance: This is easily the biggest of our bush-crickets, making it instantly recognizable by size alone. In the female (bottom), the long sword-like ovipositor (18–25 mm long) projects from the rear of the body, like a giant sting. The female uses this impressive instrument to probe into cracks in wood or in the ground, introducing the eggs into a safe place. The male (top) is slightly smaller.

Length: 40–55 mm. **Season:** June–November.

Where is it found? Usually among dense vegetation, most commonly near streams, and most abundant near the coast. This species is restricted to southern and central areas, and is absent from Ireland.

Insect facts: The very loud song can be heard from as much as 150 metres away, and can continue for hours.

Bog Bush-cricket

Scientific name: *Metrioptera brachyptera*
Family: Tettigoniidae

Appearance: This medium-sized bush-cricket is most commonly green on top and brown on the sides, but brown-topped forms also occur. The abdomen is always brown, except for the underside, which is bright green. The wing-cases are almost always very short, but fully winged forms occasionally crop up. The brown and green coloration camouflages this insect well against plants such as Cross-leaved Heath (*Erica tetralix*) on which it commonly lives.

Length: 11–20 mm. **Season:** July–October.

Where is it found? It occurs almost entirely in wet bogs on moors and heaths, but occasionally lives in drier spots as well. It crops up in scattered localities in central and southern England and Wales, but is rare in the north, and is absent from Scotland and Ireland.

Insect facts: Roesel's Bush-cricket (*Metrioptera roeseli*) looks similar, but the abdomen has a yellow underside and it lives in lush coastal grassland, not on heaths and moors.

Dark Bush-cricket

Scientific name: *Pholidoptera griseoaptera*
Family: Tettigoniidae

Appearance: This is our only common brown bush-cricket, so it cannot be mistaken for anything else. The female (illustrated) is wingless, but the male has a pair of small flap-like forewings. The underside of the abdomen is bright yellow; the female's ovipositor is quite long (10 mm) and curved upwards. The tiny nymphs rather resemble ants, and can be seen sitting around on nettles and other low plants in April and May.
Length: 13–20 mm.
Season: June–November.
Where is it found? In dense vegetation such as nettle beds and bramble patches, over the whole of south and central England and Wales. It becomes rarer in the north, and is absent from Scotland and Ireland.
Insect facts: The song of the Dark Bush-cricket is a soft chirp, repeated regularly, and often produced by several males in close company.

Yellow Sally

Scientific name: *Isoperla grammatica*
Family: Periodidae

Appearance: Stoneflies are rather drab brown or yellowish insects, with somewhat soft flattened bodies. There are usually two 'tails', or cerci, projecting from the rear end, and two pairs of wings with a complex network of veins. The Yellow Sally is the only large yellow species found in the British Isles. Male stoneflies are normally smaller than the females, as can be seen in the mating pair illustrated.
Length: 12–15 mm.
Season: April–September.
Where is it found? Beside fast-running, clear, stony streams in limestone areas.
Insect facts: Stonefly nymphs live mostly in streams or beside wave-washed lakes, where there is plenty of oxygen in the water. It usually takes a year for an egg to develop into the adult insect, which then lives only for a few days.

Common Earwig

Scientific name: *Forficula auricularia*
Family: Forficulidae

Appearance: An earwig is easily recognized by its elongate and rather flattened brown body, with a pair of pincers projecting from the rear end. This is the only earwig likely to be seen in the British Isles. The hindwings are folded in a very complicated way beneath the forewings, and can be unfurled for flight, although this is rarely seen.
Length: 10–15 mm.
Season: All year.
Where is it found? Just about anywhere; it is common in gardens.
Insect facts: Earwigs make very caring mothers. The female looks after her eggs and babies until they are able to take care of themselves. The nest is usually under a stone or log.

Birch Shieldbug

Scientific name: *Elasmostethus interstinctus*
Family: Acanthosomidae

Appearance: The head and pronotum are green, save for the rear margin of the pronotum, which is red. In the centre of the back there is a green triangle, with red surrounds. The legs are green. The Hawthorn Shieldbug (*Acanthosoma haemorrhoidale*) is very similar, but much larger (13–15 mm), and has yellowish legs.
Length: 8–10 mm.
Season: Adults April–June, August–November.
Where is it found? On birch trees wherever they occur, throughout the British Isles; it is common on birches in gardens.
Insect facts: Birch Shieldbugs feed on birches, especially the catkins, although they also sometimes feed on hazel and aspen trees. The nymph (top) is rather like a small version of the adult.

Juniper Shieldbug

Scientific name: *Cyphostethus tristriatus*
Family: Acanthosomidae

Appearance: This beautiful bug is similar to the Birch Shieldbug but, in the Juniper Shieldbug, the markings on the wing-cases are narrower, and brownish rather than red. In the middle of the back there is a yellowish blotch, which is scarcely noticeable in the Birch Shieldbug. The rather similar Hawthorn Shieldbug is easily distinguished by its larger size.

Length: 10 mm.

Season: Adult April–May, September–November.

Where are they found? This was once a rare insect, confined to scattered stands of juniper trees. In recent times, it has started to colonize cultivated *Cupressus* trees, and now occurs widely in gardens, parks, and woods throughout southern and central England and Wales.

Insect facts: Most shieldbugs hibernate as adults during the winter, and emerge in spring to mate and lay eggs. The adults then die and, for a few months, the developing nymphs are all that can be seen, until the new generation of adults appears later in the summer.

Parent Bug

Scientific name: *Elasmucha grisea*
Family: Acanthosomidae

Appearance: This small yellowish-pink shieldbug has a black-and-yellow margin around the rear two-thirds of the body. No other common British shieldbug looks at all similar. The female stands guard over her eggs and newly hatched young, and then follows her brood around and guards them while they feed. Finally, she dies shortly before her babies change into adults. The nymphs are red, black, and green, and congregate in dense family groups which look quite striking.

Length: 6 mm.

Season: May–October.

Where is it found? On birch trees throughout much of the British Isles, and sometimes on Alder (*Alnus glutinosa*).

Insect facts: Most shieldbugs, including the Parent Bug, can squirt out a very unpleasant and smelly chemical vapour when disturbed. If your nose gets too close, a whiff of this chemical can make you cough and sneeze for several minutes.

Pied Shieldbug

Scientific name: *Sehirus bicolor*
Family: Cydnidae

Appearance: This is the only black-and-white shieldbug in Britain, so cannot be mistaken for any other bug, or even for any other insect. The shiny nymphs are cream with black spots, and resemble small beetles, such as ladybirds, rather than bugs. The main foodplant is White Deadnettle (*Lamium album*), and the nymphs can usually be found feeding on its fruits. In April and May the males can often be seen chasing females across the leaves of the foodplant, after emerging from hibernation.
Length: 7–10 mm.
Season: Adults are active April–May.
Where is it found? Wherever White Deadnettle occurs, especially on roadsides, waste ground, and river banks. It is commonest in southern and central areas, but becomes rare in the north, and is absent from Scotland and Ireland.
Insect facts: The female Pied Shieldbug stands guard over her eggs in a little nest that consists of a scrape in the ground.

Woundwort Shieldbug

Scientific name: *Eysarcoris fabricii*
Family: Pentatomidae

Appearance: This small bug is pale grey and bronzy brown, with a black-and-white hind margin to the body. No other common bug looks similar. In April and May the adults emerge from hibernation, and the males begin to stridulate, making a sound inaudible to the human ear. This results in the formation of large mating aggregations, although only two mating pairs are illustrated. As in all our shieldbugs, the male and female mate in a back-to-back position.

Length: 5–6 mm.
Season: Adults visible April–October.
Where is it found? In south and central England, on roadsides, disused railway lines, and in woodland rides.
Insect facts: The normal foodplant of this bug is the Hedge Woundwort (*Stachys sylvatica*). The shiny black and yellow nymphs (quite unlike the adults) feed on the nutlets during the summer months.

Stealthy Shieldbug

Scientific name: *Troilus luridus*
Family: Pentatomidae

Appearance: This is one of two brown shieldbugs commonly found on trees. The other species, the Forest Bug (*Pentatoma rufipes*), is easily distinguished by the presence of a yellow spot almost in the middle of the back, and by square 'shoulders' (actually the edges of the pronotum). The eggs of the Stealthy Shieldbug are laid in May and June, and the nymphs (illustrated) are attractively marked in iridescent green and cream or green, red, and cream, quite unlike the drab adult coloration.

Length: 10–12 mm. **Season:** April–October.

Where is it found? On trees in woodlands and gardens, in all areas except for Scotland and the northernmost parts of Ireland.

Insect facts: This shieldbug is a hunter, stealthily approaching its prey and stabbing it with a long slim feeding-tube or rostrum. The favourite food includes moth caterpillars and soft beetle larvae.

Two-spined Shieldbug

Scientific name: *Picromerus bidens*
Family: Pentatomidae

Appearance: The spiny 'shoulders' easily distinguish this bug from our two other common brown shieldbugs, the Forest Bug (*Pentatoma rufipes*) and the Stealthy Shieldbug (*Troilus luridus*). The nymphs are dark bronzy brown, and often live in small groups. Unlike most shieldbugs, eggs are laid from August to October, after which the adults die and the small nymphs then hibernate through the winter.

Length: 12–13 mm. **Season:** Adult July–October.

Where is it found? In damp lush grassland, and in the longer grasses on downland and heathland. It is found throughout the British Isles, but becomes rarer in the north.

Insect facts: This shieldbug is a predator. It will feed on just about anything soft enough to pierce, from caterpillars and adults of moths and butterflies, to beetle larvae (as illustrated), and even on members of its own kind.

Common Green Shieldbug

Scientific name: *Palomena prasina*
Family: Pentatomidae

Appearance: This is the only completely green shieldbug found in the British Isles. Just before going into hibernation the green colour takes on a very bronzy tinge, but adults which have newly emerged from hibernation in April are a deep bright green. The nymphs are also green, but have black markings, and often form quite large groups of up to fifty individuals. These can be seen basking on the leaves of bramble and other plants in late summer.

Length: 12–14 mm.

Season: Adults April–July, September–October.

Where is it found? In woodland rides, flowery riversides, and hedgerows. This is a common insect in southern and central areas of the British Isles, but is rare in the north.

Insect facts: The Common Green Shieldbug feeds on a wide variety of trees, shrubs, and herbaceous plants, often concentrating on the fruits. The females lay eggs in batches of 14–28, producing several batches, so that the total number of eggs reaches about 100.

Gorse Shieldbug

Scientific name: *Piezodorus lituratus*
Family: Pentatomidae

Appearance: The basic coloration of this bug is green and deep yellow, with reddish antennae and yellow legs. The margins of the forewings are greyish blue. No other British bug is similar. The coloration makes this bug very hard to spot when it is sitting on the pods of gorses, (*Ulex* spp) and brooms, (*Cytisus* spp), its usual foodplants. The nymphs are an attractive shade of pinkish brown and grey.
Length: 10–12 mm.
Season: Adults April–May, August–October.
Where is it found? Throughout the British Isles, wherever gorse and broom are found, often coming into gardens to feed on ornamental brooms and lupins.
Insect facts: The eggs are laid in two neat rows of seven. The tiny newly hatched nymphs are red and black. The first meal is the old egg shell, from which the nymph takes up special symbiotic bacteria. These will remain in the bug's gut for life, and help it to digest its food.

Sloebug

Scientific name: *Dolycoris baccarum*
Family: Pentatomidae

Appearance: This shieldbug is mainly an attractive shade of pinkish brown. The triangular scutellum (in the middle of the back) is tan coloured, while the antennae and the rear margins of the body are striped in black and white. The Sloebug feeds on a wide variety of plants, but is especially fond of thistles, and it can also be abundant on garden plants such as cornflowers and knapweeds, (*Centaurea* spp), and Lamb's Tongue (*Stachys lanata*).
Length: 11–12 mm.
Season: Adults May–June, August–October.
Where is it found? Almost anywhere throughout the British Isles, but it is less common in the north.
Insect facts: During courtship the male Sloebug spends a lot of time butting his head against the underside of the female, trying to persuade her to mate with him.

Nettle Groundbug

Scientific name: *Heterogaster urticae*
Family: Lygaeidae

Appearance: The main colour of this small bug is bronzy black, and there is a black-and-white margin to the rear third of the body. It is densely hairy, although this will be obvious only when viewed with a magnifying lens. The adults emerge from hibernation in June and early July, and form large mating swarms. A small group is illustrated, in which it can be seen how the mating males and females sit in a back-to-back position.
Length: 6–7 mm.

Season: June–October.
Where is it found? Wherever Stinging Nettles occur, throughout most of mainland Britain except Scotland, and not in Ireland.
Insect facts: In this bug the act of mating can last three to four days. The female then covers the eggs with a quick-setting liquid as she lays them.

Marsh Damsel Bug

Scientific name: *Dolichonabis limbatus*
Family: Nabidae

Appearance: Damsel bugs are slim, delicate-looking insects, and there is a number of species which appear rather similar. The Marsh Damsel Bug is normally wingless, but winged forms occasionally occur. The forewings are shorter than in any other species except the Broad Damsel Bug (*Nabis flavomarginatus*). In the latter species the body tapers away backwards from its mid-point, rather than getting gradually broader, as in the Marsh Damsel Bug.

Length: 7–9 mm.

Season: August–November.

Where is it found? In the long grass of damp meadows, marshes, and marshy woodland rides, throughout the British Isles.

Insect facts: Damsel bugs are predators, feeding on other small insects, such as the nymph of the Birch Shieldbug (illustrated above).

Creeping Thistle Lacebug

Scientific name: *Tingis ampliata*
Family: Tingidae

Appearance: The pronotum (behind the head) and forewings in lacebugs are covered in hundreds of tiny punctures, giving them a rather attractive lace-like appearance, although this can really be appreciated only under a microscope. This lacebug is found only on the very common Creeping Thistle (*Cirsium arvense*). The rather similar Spear Thistle Lacebug (*Tingis cardui*) is restricted to the Spear Thistle (*Cirsium vulgare*) making it easy to distinguish between the two bugs by looking at their foodplants.

Length: 3–4 mm.

Season: May–September.

Where is it found? Wherever Creeping Thistle occurs, in south and central England.

Insect facts: Although the eggs of lacebugs are very tiny, an even tinier wasp sometimes lays its own eggs inside them.

Red-spotted Plantbug

Scientific name: *Deraeocoris ruber*
Family: Miridae

Appearance: The two red spots on the tips of the forewings are not very obvious in the female (illustrated), as she is usually reddish brown anyway, although some forms can be yellowish. By contrast, the males are generally black, so the two red spots show up well. The blackish-maroon, rather prickly nymphs are quite unlike the adults.

Length: 6–7 mm.

Season: Adults July–September.

Where is it found? On low dense vegetation, especially Stinging Nettles, over south and central England and Wales, petering out in northern England, and absent from Scotland and Ireland.

Insect facts: The Red-spotted Plantbug does not actually feed on plants, but on small insects, especially aphids.

Meadow Plantbug

Scientific name: *Leptopterna dolabrata*
Family: Miridae

Appearance: The male (illustrated) is normally black and yellow, or black and orange, and is fully winged. The greyish females look completely different and are much plumper, with very short forewings, and therefore normally flightless, although fully winged forms also occur. The legs and antennae are very hairy. The food is various types of grasses.
Length: 7–10 mm.
Season: Adults June–August.
Where is it found? On grasses throughout the British Isles.
Insect facts: The Meadow Plantbug has powerful stink glands which emit a very smelly fluid. Despite this, the bug is eaten by many kinds of spiders.

Four-spotted Oak Bug

Scientific name: *Dryophilicoris flavoquadrimaculatus*
Family: Miridae

Appearance: A broad, straight-edged, dark band towards the rear of the forewings divides them into four yellow spots (which is what '*flavoquadrimaculatus*' actually means). This bug is always found on oaks, and can often be very abundant. It feeds mainly on the unopened oak catkins, but also takes other food, such as moth eggs, aphids, small flies, and the tiny nymphs of other bugs.
Length: 6 mm.

Season: Adult May–June.
Where is it found? Only on oak trees, throughout the British Isles.
Insect facts: With thirty-four letters in its name, this bug has one of the longest scientific names of any British insect. It is beaten by an even smaller insect, the Twenty-four Spot Ladybird, which rejoices in the title of *Subcoccinella vigintiquattorpunctata* – thirty-five letters for an insect only 3 millimetres long!

Elegant Plantbug

Scientific name: *Calocoris stysi*
Family: Miridae

Appearance: This is one of our prettier and more conspicuous plantbugs, and it is often very common. There is a distinctive yellowish-orange triangle towards the tip of each forewing. The main food consists of nettle catkins, in bud and in fruit, but this bug also sucks the sap of many other plants, and feeds on other small, soft-bodied insects, such as aphids.
Length: 6–8 mm.
Season: Adult June–August.
Where is it found? Throughout the British Isles in suitable habitats, on nettles and other low plants in woods, on roadsides, and riverbanks, etc.
Insect facts: The female Elegant Plantbug does not lay her eggs in the nettles on which the nymphs will feed, but instead inserts them into crevices in the bark of nearby trees and bushes.

Striped Oak Bug

Scientific name: *Calocoris quadripunctatus*
Family: Miridae

Appearance: There are two yellow marks towards the tips of the forewings, which also bear longitudinal stripes. These stripes, however, are not as straight and neat as in the similar Large Striped Plantbug (*see* below), which also has a much more parallel-sided outline. In the Striped Oak Bug the body shape is rather more rounded, with gently curving sides.
Length: 7–8 mm.
Season: Adult May–July.
Where is it found? On oak throughout the British Isles.
Insect facts: The nymphs of this bug feed mainly on the developing oak catkins in springtime. The adults' diet consists chiefly of other insects, such as small bug nymphs and aphids.

Large Striped Plantbug

Scientific name: *Miris striatus*
Family: Miridae

Appearance: This is by far the largest of our plantbugs, and is also one of the most handsome. It gets its name from the narrow, longitudinal, dark-brown and yellow stripes along the forewings. There is also a yellowish-orange triangular mark near the tip of each forewing. The nymphs are dark reddish brown or black, with yellow markings. The only other similar bug is illustrated above.

Length: 9–11 mm.
Season: Adult May–June.
Where is it found? On a wide range of trees, but especially on oak and hawthorn, throughout the British Isles, but more commonly in the north.
Insect facts: The Large Striped Plantbug feeds mainly on insect eggs and soft-bodied insects, such as aphids and small caterpillars.

Water Measurer

Scientific name: *Hydrometra stagnorum*
Family: Hydrometridae

Appearance: This rather sombre, blackish, wingless insect is one of our thinnest bugs. It moves around slowly on its slim, stilt-like legs among waterside vegetation, and on the surfaces of ponds and lakes, searching for small prey to skewer with its beak (rostrum).
Length: 9–11 mm.
Season: May–August.
Where is it found? Beside ponds, lakes, rivers, and ditches throughout the British Isles.
Insect facts: A hunting Water Measurer can detect the tiny vibrations made by underwater creatures, such as mosquito larvae. The hunter then plunges its rostrum down through the water, to spear the prey on its tip.

Toothed Pondskater

Scientific name: *Gerris odontogaster*
Family: Gerridae

Appearance: Like all pondskaters, this bug moves easily across the surface of open water, supported on its middle and rear pairs of legs. Where these make contact with the water's surface film, there are four small dimples. The front legs are not used for support, but serve for catching prey. Most pondskaters have short wings or none at all, and cannot fly, but fully winged forms do occur.

Length: 10–12 mm.

Season: May–October.

Where is it found? On ponds, canals, and lakes throughout the British Isles.

Insect facts: Pondskaters often feed on insects and spiders that have fallen into the water and are floundering helplessly on its surface. Pondskaters, however, are not afraid to attack strong and vigorous insects that are at home near water, such as the damselfly in the illustration.

Water Scorpion

Scientific name: *Nepa cinerea*
Family: Nepidae

Appearance: This harmless bug's name comes from its scorpion-like appearance, with a 'tail' at the rear end (actually a breathing tube for tapping air from the surface) and large, powerful, scorpion-like front legs (used for grasping prey). The prey can include quite large creatures, such as tadpoles and baby fishes. Water Scorpions are fully winged but seldom fly, and are usually seen trundling around on muddy pond margins.

Length: 15 mm.
Season: All year.
Where is it found? Throughout the British Isles, in all kinds of water.
Insect facts: The Water Scorpion lays its eggs in masses of green algae, or inside the stems and leaves of water plants. When handled, it pretends to be dead, and it has small extra hearts in its wings to promote the circulation of its body fluid.

Horned Treehopper

Scientific name: *Centrotus cornutus*
Family: Membracidae

Appearance: With two small horns sticking out from either side of the pronotum, this is like no other British insect. The pronotum also bears a rather wavy rearwards extension, that almost reaches the tip of the body. The transparent wings are suffused with brown, and bear a network of prominent brown veins.

Length: 8–9 mm.
Season: Adult May–July.
Where is it found? On tree saplings, bushes, and plants such as willowherbs, over much of the British Isles.
Insect facts: The nymphs of this hopper are rarely seen, as they lurk at the bases of plants, where they are often partly covered by soil or dead leaves.

Common Froghopper

Scientific name: *Philaenus spumarius*
Family: Cercopidae

Appearance: A mating pair of adults is illustrated, sitting in the side-by-side position typical of mating hoppers. The colour of the adult is brownish, blackish, or reddish, usually with some paler markings, but it is always very variable.

Length: 6 mm.

Season: Adults June–September; nymphs April–July.

Where is it found? In grassy and bushy places throughout the British Isles.

Insect facts: Another name for this bug is the Cuckoo Spit Bug. This is because the nymph lives inside a mass of froth (*see* illustration), which squirts out of the nymph's rear end. This white foamy blob prevents the very soft-bodied occupant from drying out.

Black and Red Froghopper

Scientific name: *Cercopis vulnerata*
Family: Cercopidae

Appearance: The only other black and red British insects that are remotely similar are some ladybirds, but they are dome shaped rather than tent shaped as this bug is; it has six large red spots on a black background. Like all froghoppers, it leaps away when disturbed. When mating, the bugs sit side by side (illustrated). The black and red colours warn that this bug has an unpleasant flavour.
Length: 8–12 mm.
Season: April–August.
Where is it found? In bushy and grassy places.
Insect facts: The nymphs of this froghopper live on roots below ground, surrounded by a substantial mass of solidified foam.

Nettle Aphid

Scientific name: *Microlaphium carnosum*
Family: Aphididae

Appearance: This bright-green aphid is normally covered with a mealy-whitish coating, which gives it a pale bluish-green appearance. During summer the females give birth to a succession of live offspring, so that the nettles soon become covered in thousands of busily feeding aphids. Two tiny black 'horns', called cornicles, project upwards from the rear end and secrete wax.
Length: 2 mm.
Season: May–July.
Where is it found? On nettles throughout the British Isles.
Insect facts: During the summer months all the live offspring produced by an aphid are female, and these go on to turn out more and more babies, without ever mating. In autumn the aphids begin to produce males, which mate with the females, which then lay large eggs. These eggs are tough enough to pass the winter in the open.

Green Tiger Beetle

Scientific name: *Cicindela campestris*
Family: Carabidae

Appearance: This is the only reasonably large and spectacular, bright-green ground beetle in the British Isles, so it cannot be mistaken for any other insect. The yellow spots on the wing-cases are variable in size, shape, and number. It runs very fast and flies readily when disturbed, but soon lands again. The large jaws are used for seizing prey and tearing it to pieces.
Length: 10–15 mm.
Season: April–September, but commonest April–May.
Where is it found? On heathlands and other sandy places.
Insect facts: The larva of the Green Tiger Beetle lives in a vertical burrow in the ground. The larva's mouth is so huge that, with jaws agape, it completely blocks the burrow's entrance. When an insect walks past, the larva darts out and grabs it.

Rough-backed Ground Beetle

Scientific name: *Carabus granulatus*
Family: Carabidae

Appearance: This is the only large, rough-backed, blackish-bronze ground beetle that is common in the British Isles. The very common Violet Ground Beetle (*Carabus violaceus*) is much smoother and shinier, and a lovely violet sheen ripples across its black coloration when it moves. Most ground beetles are flightless, but they are fast runners.
Length: 17–23 mm.
Season: April–September.
Where is it found? Running around on the ground in grassy places and woodlands, throughout the British Isles.
Insect facts: Large ground beetles, such as this one, feed mainly at night on rather soft-bodied prey, particularly worms and slugs.

Devil's Coach-horse Beetle

Scientific name: *Ocypus olens*
Family: Staphylinidae

Appearance: When threatened, this inky black beetle turns the rear end of its body upwards (*see* illustration), giving rise to the alternative name of Cock-tail Beetle. Note the large gaping jaws (a nip from these can hurt), and the tiny wing-cases, which cover only the front third of the abdomen. This is the only large black beetle of its type that is common in the British Isles.

Length: 22–32 mm.
Season: Active all summer.
Where is it found? Just about anywhere in the British Isles.
Insect facts: The Devil's Coach-horse usually spends the day under logs and stones, emerging at night to hunt worms and slugs, which it tears apart with its huge jaws.

Stag Beetle

Scientific name: *Lucanus cervus*
Family: Lucanidae

Appearance: This is our biggest beetle, so size alone is enough to prevent confusion with any other species. The males have the huge, protruding pincer-like jaws seen in the illustration. The female's jaws are much smaller. The males use their huge jaws as 'antlers' in fights, levering one another up off a dead tree or stump. Adults of both sexes lick sap oozing from wounded trees.
Length: Male 25–75 mm; female 30–45 mm.
Season: On the wing May–September.
Where is it found? Very locally in southern England. It is most common just south of London, and even into the outer suburbs.
Insect facts: The Stag Beetle larva is a huge, fat, white grub which lives inside decaying oak stumps. It takes five years to develop.

Bumble-dor Beetle

Scientific name: *Geotrupes stercorarius*
Family: Geotrupidae

Appearance: This very rounded beetle is shiny black on top, and a lovely metallic blue or green on the underside. Seven narrow grooves run from front to rear of each wing-case. The pronotum is smooth, and the black legs are very spiny. *Aphodius rufipes* is also found on dung, but is smaller (9–13 mm), and has a broad plate-like head and reddish-brown legs.
Length: 15–25 mm.
Season: April–October.
Where is it found? In pastures and woodlands over most of the British Isles.
Insect facts: The Bumble-dor gathers dung and buries it in shafts in the ground, often beneath cow pats. The dung then functions as a larder for the developing larvae.

Cockchafer Beetle

Scientific name: *Melolontha melolontha*
Family: Scarabaeidae

Appearance: This is much the largest of several mainly brown chafers found in Britain. The thorax is black and the wing-cases are light brown, with the tip of the abdomen protruding as a point beyond them. The male (illustrated) has quite large fan-like antennae. These are much smaller in the female, which is also larger. Cockchafers fly at night, but in daytime can sometimes be found sitting on leaves or flowers.
Length: 20–30 mm.
Season: May–July.
Where is it found? Just about anywhere, including gardens in large towns.
Insect facts: The Cockchafer larva is a large fat grub which spends four years underground, eating the roots of grasses and other plants. It can be a serious pest, killing crops and garden plants. The Cockchafer is also commonly called the Maybug though, of course, it is not a true bug.

Garden Chafer Beetle

Scientific name: *Phyllopertha horticola*
Family: Scarabaeidae

Appearance: The wing-cases of this rather hairy beetle are a shiny brown, while the head and pronotum are a deep metallic green. The antennae are divided into three flaps. In other similar chafers, the head and thorax are dark greyish or brownish. The beetle illustrated is feeding on a Dog Rose (*Rosa canina*). Flowers and leaves are the main diet of the adult beetles. Garden chafers fly by day, and can be very common where they occur, although this is often in very scattered localities.
Length: 7–12 mm.
Season: April–July; commonest in June.
Where is it found? Mostly in bushy grasslands (rare in gardens, despite its name), over much of the British Isles.
Insect facts: The fully grown larva is 23 mm long and lives in the soil, where it eats roots. It takes only one year to develop.

Click Beetle

Scientific name: *Denticollis linearis*
Family: Elateridae

Appearance: The pronotum is distinctly humped and considerably narrower than the wing-cases, a very unusual feature in click beetles. The light-brown wing cases are abundantly furrowed from front to rear. The antennae are rather long, and bear numerous antler-like projections. The black head is more prominent than in most similar species. The larvae are predators and inhabit rotting wood, such as fallen trees.

Length: 9–12 mm (excluding antennae).
Season: June–August.
Where is it found? Mostly in woodlands.
Insect facts: By using a special hinged mechanism, a Click Beetle stranded on its back can snap the two parts of its body backwards, giving such an explosive release of tension that the beetle is propelled into the air.

Soldier Beetle

Scientific name: *Rhagonycha fulva*
Family: Cantharidae

Appearance: This is by far the commonest of our soldier beetles, and it often occurs in huge numbers on flowers. The wing-cases are tipped with black, and the pronotum is almost square. In the similar and rather bigger (10–14 mm) *Cantharis livida*, the wing-cases are not black tipped, and the pronotum is broader than it is long. Soldier beetles spend a lot of time on flowers, feeding on small insects and pollen.

Length: 9–10 mm.
Season: June–September; commonest July–August.
Where is it found? Just about anywhere in the British Isles.
Insect facts: Whenever you find soldier beetles, they always seem to be mating. This is because the males try to stay with the females as long as possible, keeping other males away until just before the females lay their eggs.

Red-headed Cardinal Beetle

Scientific name: *Pyrochroa serraticornis*
Family: Pyrochroidae

Appearance: Except for the black antennae and legs, this handsome beetle is a bright rusty red. The similar and less common Cardinal Beetle (*Pyrochroa coccinea*) is a brighter, purer red and has a black head. In both species the antennae are abundantly toothed. Cardinal beetles are fond of flowers such as buttercups, but also occur on tree trunks, where they lap up oozing sap.
Length: 15–20 mm.
Season: May–July.
Where is it found? In lush flowery places, such as woodland edges, damp roadsides, and riverbanks, throughout most of the British Isles.
Insect facts: Cardinal beetle larvae live under the loose bark of dead and dying trees, preying upon other small creatures which live there.

Red-tipped Grass Beetle

Scientific name: *Malachius bipustulatus*
Family: Malachiidae

Appearance: The top of the pronotum and the wing-cases are shining blackish green. The wing-cases have conspicuous red tips, and the underside of the abdomen is also red. The top of the abdomen, where it protrudes from beneath the wing-cases at the rear end, is black with two transverse white stripes. The adults are usually found on the heads of flowering grasses, while the larvae live under bark.

Length: 5–6 mm.
Season: May–June.
Where is it found? This beetle is widespread but local, in damp flowery places, especially on river banks.
Insect facts: At the bases of the male's antennae there are special glands on which the female nibbles during courtship.

Seven-spot Ladybird

Scientific name: *Coccinella septempunctata*
Family: Coccinellidae

Appearance To identify this, the commonest of our ladybirds, just count the seven black spots on the wing-cases. The wing-cases are pale orange in adults which have recently emerged from pupae, but become much redder with age. The larva's bluish-grey body tapers from front to back, and is blotched with pale orange. It is not shiny like the adult.

Length: 5–9 mm.

Season: Adults emerge from hibernation (which often takes place in swarms) in April and May, and lay eggs. The new generation of adults appears in July.

Where is it found? Just about anywhere in the British Isles.

Insect facts: The adults and larvae of most ladybirds, including this one, feed on aphids.

Two-spot Ladybird

Scientific name: *Adalia bipunctata*
Family: Coccinellidae

Appearance: The colour and pattern of this ladybird are very variable. The two most common forms are depicted in the mating pair in the illustration. The female has two black spots on a red background, but in the male this is reversed, with two red spots on a black background. Some forms have more than two spots, others have blotches or bands of colour, while some have no pattern at all.
Length: 3–5 mm.
Season: As in Seven-spot Ladybird (*see* above).
Where is it found? Everywhere, as far north as southern Scotland.
Insect facts: If they are roughly handled, the larvae and adults of ladybirds can exude an evil-tasting yellow liquid. This prevents enemies, such as birds, from eating them.

Ten-spot Ladybird

Scientific name: *Adalia decempunctata*
Family: Coccinellidae

Appearance: This small ladybird usually has five variably sized black spots on each pale-orange wing-case. There are five more black spots on the pronotum, just behind the head. The colour and pattern are very variable, however, and some forms are yellow with black spots, while others are black, with just two orange spots.

Length: 3–5 mm.

Season: April–August.

Where is it found? Mostly on trees in woodlands and hedgerows, almost everywhere.

Insect facts: The bright colours of ladybirds serve to warn about their nasty tasting defensive secretions. Birds and other enemies then learn to recognize ladybirds by their pattern alone, and do not touch them.

Eyed Ladybird

Scientific name: *Anatis ocellata*
Family: Coccinellidae

Appearance: The wing-cases are a rather pale brownish orange, marked with seven or eight black spots. Each of these is usually surrounded by a pale-yellowish ring, although this is often missing. There are two white blotches on the rear edge of the pronotum, which usually has a broad white border to either side. This is the biggest British ladybird.

Length: 8–9 mm.

Season: Adults are most often seen July–September.

Where is it found? On pine trees throughout the British Isles.

Insect facts: Although normally living on pine trees, where it eats aphids, the Eyed Ladybird can also be found sitting on plants, such as bracken, below the trees.

Fourteen-spot Ladybird

Scientific name: *Propylea 14-punctata*
Family: Coccinellidae

Appearance: As in several other ladybirds, the pattern in this species is very variable. Usually there are seven more-or-less rectangular black blotches on each wing-case. Some forms are almost entirely black, while others are almost completely yellow.
Length: 5–7 mm.
Season: Active all summer.
Where is it found? Almost anywhere.
Insect facts: The Twenty-two-spot Ladybird (*Psyllobora 22-punctata*) is also small and yellow, but this is more of a lemon yellow, and it has twenty-two black spots.

Varied Carpet Beetle

Scientific name: *Anthrenus verbasci*
Family: Dermestidae

Appearance: The adult beetle looks like a tiny brownish-grey ladybird, but with pale zig-zag lines across the wing-cases, rather than spots. The larva (illustrated) is more often seen than the adult, and is a strange bristly creature with a pair of prominent tail-tufts.
Length: 2–3 mm.

Season: All year.
Where is it found? Mainly inside buildings, but the normal habitat is birds' nests.
Insect facts: The larva of this beetle eats feathers and woollen materials, so it can be a pest in houses, eating carpets and clothes. It can also do great damage to animal collections in museums. The adults eat pollen.

Thick-legged Flower Beetle

Scientific name: *Oedemera nobilis*
Family: Oedemeridae

Appearance: The males and females of this beetle are a bright metallic green. While the rather more slender females could be mistaken for one or two other similar beetles, however, the more sturdy males are unmistakable because of their very swollen hind legs. Note how the wing-cases splay outwards towards the rear, exposing the hindmost part of the abdomen.
Length: 8–10 mm.
Season: May–August.
Where is it found? In all kinds of flowery places over most of England and Wales, although always very scattered.
Insect facts: The larvae of this beetle live inside the stems of plants.

Oil Beetle

Scientific name: *Meloe proscarabaeus*
Family: Meloidae

Appearance: The female (illustrated, eating a leaf) is a fat and rather sausage-shaped black beetle with very short, gaping wing-cases, which appear to be rather a tight fit for the bulging abdomen. The male is smaller. When molested, Oil Beetles release an evil-smelling and nasty tasting defensive oily liquid.
Length: Male 10–25 mm; female 25–30 mm.
Season: April–July.
Where is it found? In grassy places.
Insect facts: Oil Beetles lay thousands of eggs. The larvae sit on flowers and wait for a solitary bee to arrive. They hitch-hike back to the nest on the bee, and then kill its larva and eat its food stores of pollen and nectar.

Wasp Beetle

Scientific name: *Clytus arietis*
Family: Cerambycidae

Appearance: No other British beetle has the wasp-like black-and-yellow stripes seen in this beetle. The antennae are unusually short for a member of this family (the longhorn beetles), but are a perfect match for the antennae of a wasp. Even this beetle's movements are very jerky and wasp-like. It is found on a great variety of flowers.
Length: 7–15 mm (excluding antennae).
Season: May–July.
Where is it found? In woodland rides, wooded roadsides, disused railway lines, and gardens, throughout the British Isles.
Insect facts: Wasp Beetle larvae develop inside small-diameter dead timber; bean-sticks in gardens are sometimes used.

Spotted Longhorn Beetle

Scientific name: *Strangalia maculata*
Family: Cerambycidae

Appearance: This is another vaguely wasp-like beetle, but its antennae (which are black, with narrow yellow rings) are much longer than in the Wasp Beetle, and the Spotted Longhorn is usually much bigger. The pattern of black and yellow is extremely variable but, in Britain, any beetle looking similar to the illustration will be this species, unless it has totally black antennae. In the latter case, it will be the Four-banded Longhorn (*Strangalia quadrifasciata*). A more square-bodied, much shorter look-alike will be *Judolia cerambyciformis*.

Length: 14–20 mm (excluding antennae).
Season: June–August.
Where is it found? Usually on flowers, in woodland rides, hedgerows, and along roadsides, throughout the British Isles.
Insect facts: The larvae of this beetle occur in rotting tree stumps.

Large Flower Longhorn Beetle

Scientific name: *Stenocorus meridianus*
Family: Cerambycidae

Appearance: Although the beetle illustrated has brown wing-cases, these can also be black. The antennae are nearly as long as the body, and they are even longer in the male than in the female illustrated. This beetle is normally found feeding on flowers, especially Hogweed [*Heracleum sphondylium* (illustrated)] and Dog Rose (*Rosa canina*).
Length: 15–25 mm (excluding antennae).
Season: May–June.
Where is it found? On woodland borders in southern and central areas of England and Wales.
Insect facts: The larvae of this beetle live inside diseased trees such as oak and beech.

Back-slash Longhorn Beetle

Scientific name: *Rhagium bifasciatum*
Family: Cerambycidae

Appearance: The wing-cases of this beetle are mainly blackish brown, with four pale-yellowish, backward-slanting stripes, like back-slashes. It is normally found feeding on flowers such as Dog Roses [*Rose canina* (illustrated)]. The larvae usually live inside conifer trees.
Length: 12–22 mm.
Season: May–August.
Where is it found? In woodland rides, over most of the British Isles except for Scotland, but always very locally.
Insect facts: The females of this beetle can be quite rough with the males, and sometimes bite off their antennae or legs.

Pond Leaf Beetle

Scientific name: *Plateumaris sericea*
Family: Chrysomelidae

Appearance: This is rather an elongate beetle, superficially similar to various soldier beetles (Cantharidae), but much more metallic. The colour is very variable, as can be seen by the mating pair illustrated, which comprise a blue male and a bronzy brown female. Greenish and reddish forms are also common. Numerous species of *Donacia* are very similar, and can be distinguished only by an expert. In all these beetles the males have moderately swollen hindlegs.
Length: 6–8 mm.
Season: May–July.
Where is it found? By ponds, lakes, and slow-moving rivers, over most of the British Isles.
Insect facts: Pond Leaf Beetle larvae live under water, and breathe by tapping into the air supplies of aquatic plants.

Bloody-nosed Beetle

Scientific name: *Timarcha tenebricosa*
Family: Chrysomelidae

Appearance: As can be seen from the illustration, this beetle gets its name from its ability to ooze a droplet of red 'blood' from its mouth. It does this only when it is severely mishandled. The wing-cases of this shiny black beetle are fused together, making flight impossible. The sides of the pronotum slope inwards towards the rear. The shiny blue-black larvae and the adults feed on bedstraws (*Galium* spp).
Length: 10–20 mm.
Season: April–August.
Where is it found? In rough grassy and bushy places, such as roadsides and woodland edges, over most of the British Isles.
Insect facts: *Timarcha goettingensis* is similar, but is rather duller and smaller, and the pronotum has almost parallel sides.

Mint Leaf Beetle

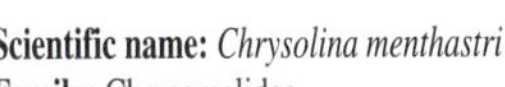

Scientific name: *Chrysolina menthastri*
Family: Chrysomelidae

Appearance: This is the only deep metallic green leaf beetle likely to occur on mints, which is where you are almost certain to find this species. The body is more rounded at the front and rear, compared with the chopped-off appearance of the species described below.
Length: 10 mm.
Season: May–September.
Where is it found? Almost anywhere on mints, including in gardens, where it can be a pest.
Insect facts: The Poplar Leaf Beetle (*Crysomela populi*) has bright reddish-brown wing-cases and a blackish-green head and pronotum. It feeds on willows and poplars. *Chrysolina polita* is a smaller, dark brownish-red beetle, with a green head and pronotum. It is common in damp places.

Leaf Beetle

Scientific name: *Cryptocephalus aureolus*
Family: Chrysomelidae

Appearance: This is a squat little beetle, with very blunt front and rear ends, apparently chopped off short. The thorax and wing-cases are bright metallic green, covered in hundreds of tiny puncture marks. The adults are usually found on flowers, especially on yellow-flowered members of the daisy family, such as *Hypochoeris* spp and *Hieracium* spp. There are several more similar beetles in the same genus.
Length: 5–7 mm.
Season: June–August.
Where is it found? In grassy places.
Insect facts: The larvae live inside little cases and feed on dead leaves.

Pot-bellied Emerald Beetle

Scientific name: *Gastrophysa viridula*
Family: Chrysomelidae

Appearance: The male and female of this beetle are a bright metallic green. The females soon develop a remarkably swollen abdomen, so that the wing-cases perched on top look much too small. The adults, and the black larvae, both feed on docks (*Rumex* spp). These can rapidly be reduced to tatters by the inroads made by hordes of tiny mouths.

Size: 4–5 mm.
Season: May–August.
Where is it found? On dock plants throughout most of the British Isles, but always rather locally distributed.
Insect facts: The bright-yellow eggs of this beetle are laid in batches of ten to twenty The empty egg shells comprise the first meal for the newly hatched larvae.

Thistle Tortoise Beetle

Scientific name: *Cassida rubiginosa*
Family: Chrysomelidae

Appearance: Although it is usually plain green, this beetle can also be marked with gold or black, and some forms are reddish brown. The hind margin of the pronotum, where it bends inwards from either side, is angled, whereas in the similar Mint Tortoise Beetle (*Cassida viridis*) this bend is curved. The latter species is also a brighter green, bigger (8–10 mm), and is found only on mints and related plants.
Length: 6–8 mm.
Season: May–October.
Where is it found? Just about anywhere on thistles and burdock.
Insect facts: The tortoise beetle larva holds a little bundle of droppings over its back, as protection from enemies.

Hazel Leaf Roller Weevil

Scientific name: *Apoderus coryli*
Family: Attelabidae

Appearance: The colour of this insect varies from a pale, rusty orange to a deep, bright red. The front part of the head is black, and the head is very narrow at the rear, with a distinct 'neck'. The similar-looking Red Oak Roller (*Attelabus nitens*) has a thick-set, totally black head, with no 'neck', and lives on oaks.
Length: 6–7 mm.
Season: May–September.
Where is it found? Just about anywhere on hazel trees, but also quite common on birches.
Insect facts: The female of this beetle rolls up a hazel or birch leaf as a 'cradle' for her larvae. These leaf-rolls are very easy to spot, because they go brown before the rest of the leaves on the tree.

Vine Weevil

Scientific name: *Otiorhynchus sulcatus*
Family: Curculionidae

Appearance: This bronzy black weevil is usually covered with tiny tufts of yellowish scales, but these soon wear off, leaving a plain blackish appearance.
Length: 8–10 mm.
Season: All year.
Where is it found? Mainly in houses and gardens, throughout the British Isles.
Insect facts. Vine Weevil larvae are fat white grubs, which are a pest of garden and house plants. The latter are often killed as a result of the damage done to their roots by numerous Vine Weevil larvae, feeding undetected in the soil. These larvae are very resistant to insecticides.

Silvery Green Tree Weevil

Scientific name: *Phyllobius argentatus*
Family: Curculionidae

Appearance: The body is thickly covered with shining golden-green scales, giving it an overall silvery appearance. The legs and antennae are reddish beneath the scales, which soon rub off in older specimens; the one illustrated is very fresh.

Length: 4–6 mm.
Season: June–August.
Where is it found? Usually on trees, but sometimes on vegetation growing beneath them, throughout the British Isles.
Insect facts: *Phyllobius pomaceus* is slightly larger (7–9 mm) and less silvery, and is common on nettles. There are ten species of *Phyllobius* in Britain, most of them living on trees.

Large Figwort Weevil

Scientific name: *Cionus scrophulariae*
Family: Curculionidae

Appearance: With its black-and-white, blotchy appearance, this miniature weevil rather resembles a small bird-dropping. There is a black spot in the centre of the back, looking very like a hole in the weevil's body. Several other similar species occur on figworts, but all are smaller than this one.
Length: 4–5 mm.
Season: May–August.
Where is it found? On figwort plants (*Scrophularia* spp), wherever they grow, on roadsides, woodland edges, riverbanks etc., throughout the British Isles.
Insect facts: *Cionus* larvae are shiny, mucus-covered, slug-like creatures. They pupate in a spherical, papery brown cocoon at the top of the plant, among the seed pods, which the cocoons mimic, making them hard to spot.

Red Dock Weevil

Scientific name: *Apion miniatum*
Family: Curculionidae

Appearance: The body is entirely red, and the front end is characteristically pointed. A series of grooves runs from front to back on each wing-case. There are several other reddish species, which are difficult to distinguish, but do not live on dock plants.
Length: 3–4 mm.
Season: May–June.
Where is it found? On dock plants, wherever they occur.
Insect facts: *Apion* weevils are often attributed to their own separate family, the Apionidae.

Grey Oak Weevil

Scientific name: *Curculio villosus*
Family: Curculionidae

Appearance: The body is blotched with grey and white. The 'snout', or rostrum, is long, and curves downwards. The Acorn Weevil (*Curculio glandium*) is larger (5–8 mm) and brown, and also occurs on oaks, but its larvae develop inside the acorns.
Length: 4–5 mm.
Season: May–August.
Where is it found? On oaks throughout the British Isles.
Insect facts: The larvae of this weevil develop inside the galls (special swellings) caused by the larvae of certain wasps on oaks.

Common Goldeneye Lacewing

Scientific name: *Chrysopa carnea*
Family: Chrysopidae

Appearance: This bright-green lacewing, with its shining golden eyes, is one of several similar-looking species which are all very common. Unlike *Chrysopa pallens*, it does not have six black dots on the head. In *Chrysopa perla* the body is bluish green, rather than bright green, and the head and body are heavily marked with black.
Length: 14–17 mm.
Season: All year, often overwintering in houses.
Where is it found? Just about anywhere, throughout the British Isles.
Insect facts: Green lacewing eggs are laid at the tips of long stalks. The larvae feed on aphids.

Alder Fly

Scientific name: *Sialis lutaria*
Family: Sialidae

Appearance: The adult Alder Fly is easily recognized by its smoky brown wings, with their open network of thick black veins. When not in use, the wings are folded tent-like above the back. The antennae are long and thin. The adults seldom feed, and are usually seen sitting on waterside vegetation. The larva is an aquatic predator.
Length: 15–20 mm.
Season: April–August.
Where is it found? Beside ponds and lakes throughout the British Isles.
Insect facts: Alder Flies lay their eggs in batches of several hundred on waterside plants. Several females will often choose the same leaf, building up huge masses containing thousands of eggs.

Common Snakefly

Scientific name: *Raphidia notata*
Family: Raphidiidae

Appearance: A snakefly can be easily recognized by its long 'neck', which gives it an appearance quite unlike that of any other British insect. The transparent wings, with their prominent black veins, are stowed alongside the body. In the female (illustrated), a spike-like ovipositor protrudes from the rear end.
Length: 15–20 mm.
Season: May–July.
Where is it found? Rather locally, on and near oaks.
Insect facts: This snakefly lays its eggs under oak bark. Its larvae prey on other small creatures beneath the bark. Other snakefly species lay their eggs on pines.

Giant Horntail

Scientific name: *Urocerus gigas*
Family: Siricidae

Appearance: The female (illustrated) of this large insect has a fearsome appearance, with her black-and-yellow, wasp-like pattern, and long ovipositor spike protruding from the rear end, like a giant sting. In fact, she is completely harmless, and the ovipositor is used for drilling into pine trees, as shown in the illustration, to lay eggs within the timber. The male is much smaller, and the tip of his abdomen is black.

Length: 30–50 mm.

Season: May–October.

Where is it found? In pine woods throughout the British Isles.

Insect facts: When the female lays her eggs in the pine tree, she introduces a special fungus. This infects the tunnels in which the larvae develop, and helps to pre-digest the wood.

Large Rose Sawfly

Scientific name: *Arge pagana*
Family: Argidae

Appearance: The pronotum, abdomen, and legs of this sawfly are all bright golden yellow. The wings are dark yellowish. The body is rather short and squat. The females can usually be found perched on Dog Rose (*Rosa canina*) cutting egg-laying slits with their saw-like ovipositors.

Length: 7–10 mm.

Season: June–September.

Where is it found? In woodland rides, along hedgerows, on disused railway lines, and on roadsides, wherever wild roses occur. It is restricted to southern and central England, but is often common within that area.

Insect facts: The larvae of this sawfly are attractive, pale-green, caterpillar-like creatures, covered with black spots. They always occur in groups, and often reduce the roses to shreds.

Sawfly

Scientific name: *Tenthredo temula*
Family: Tenthredinidae

Appearance: Though reasonably wasp-like, the resemblance is less convincing than in the next species. The tops of the head and pronotum are black. Most of the abdomen is also black, but segment 3, the sides of segments 4 and 5, and the middles of segments 6 to 9, are yellow. This species is usually found on flowers, especially Hogweed (*Heracleum sphondylium*).
Length: 10–12 mm.
Season: May–June.
Where is it found? On lanesides, woodland borders, riverbanks etc., throughout the British Isles, except for the far north of Scotland.

Figwort Sawfly

Scientific name: *Tenthredo scrophulariae*
Family: Tenthredinidae

Appearance: Although several kinds of common British sawflies have a wasp-like, black-and-yellow pattern, this is by far the most convincing. It is only by a close inspection that its true identity can be established. Note the absence of the slim, wasp-like 'waist', connecting the abdomen to the thorax. The bright yellowish-orange antennae serve to distinguish this species from any other black-and-yellow sawflies.
Length: 10–15 mm.
Season: May–August.
Where is it found? Throughout the British Isles.
Insect facts: The adults can often be found flying around figwort plants (*Scrophularia* spp), on which their black-spotted, powdery white larvae develop. Mulleins (*Verbascum* spp) are also sometimes used.

Lime-green Sawfly

Scientific name: *Tenthredo mesomelas*
Family Tenthredinidae

Appearance: This is much the commonest of our green sawflies, although the green always has a yellowish tinge to it. Note that the head and the top of the thorax are almost completely black, and the top of the abdomen is heavily marked with black bands. There is less black in the common Apple-green Sawfly (*Rhogogaster viridis*) which is also a purer shade of green, lacking the yellow tinge.
Length: 10–13 mm.
Season: May–July.
Where is it found? Among dense vegetation in woods and marshes, and on riverbanks and roadsides, throughout the British Isles.

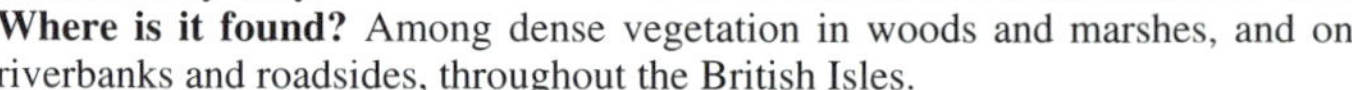

Insect facts: This sawfly is a predator. It jumps upon other insects and tears them apart with its jaws.

Banner Wasp

Scientific name: *Gasteruption assectator*
Family: Gasteruptiidae

Appearance: The female of this wasp is unmistakable, with her long slim body and equally long, spine-like ovipositor, which has a conspicuous white tip. When the wasp is in flight, the long back legs are trailed downwards to the rear (*see* illustration). Both sexes are often found on flowers.

Length: 30–40 mm.
Season: June–August.
Where is it found? On flowers in dry grassy places and old quarries, and on heaths and sand-dunes.
Insect facts: Banner Wasp females use their long ovipositors to lay eggs deep inside the nests of solitary bees. The wasp larva eats the bee larva, and then tucks into its store of food.

Sabre Wasp

Scientific name: *Rhyssa persuasoria*
Family: Ichneumonidae

Appearance: This impressive insect is easily recognized by its length alone. The black body is liberally sprinkled with white blotches; the legs are mainly orange and the antennae are black. In the females, a long, slender, almost hair-like ovipositor projects from the rear end, and is about the same length as the body.

Length: Females up to 85 mm.

Season: June–September.

Where is it found? Wherever conifers grow, throughout the British Isles.

Insect facts: Although the ovipositor looks soft and flexible, it is able to penetrate deeply into solid pine wood, to parasitize the larva of the Giant Horntail (*Urocerus gigas*) living within.

Ruby-tailed Wasp

Scientific name: *Chrysis ignita*
Family: Chrysididae

Appearance: The body of this attractive, metallic, jewel-like wasp is very heavily pitted. The head and thorax are green from one angle and blue from another, or a mixture of the two, depending on the angle of the light reflected from the body. The abdomen is a bright ruby red. There are several other similar-looking species. The females are usually found on dead trees, fence posts, sandy banks, etc., wherever the nest holes of solitary wasps are likely to occur. They also feed on flowers, especially the umbels of Hogweed (*Heracleum sphondylium*) and Wild Angelica (*Angelica sylvestris*).

Length: 5–15 mm.

Season: April–September.

Where is it found? In most habitats, including gardens.

Insect facts: The larvae develop as 'cuckoos' inside the nests of solitary wasps.

Black Garden Ant

Scientific name: *Lasius niger*
Family: Formicidae

Appearance: This is the only one of our numerous species of black ants that is at all common in towns and gardens. The colour is often dark brown rather than pure black. The nests are frequently found beneath stones, especially flagstones. The nuptial flight of the fully winged males and females (illustrated) takes place in July and August, usually from hundreds of nests simultaneously.
Length: Female 8–9 mm; male and worker 3–5 mm.
Season: All year, but it hibernates in dense clusters under stones in winter.
Where is it found? Just about anywhere.
Insect facts: The winged females or queens break off their wings soon after they have mated.

Yellow Meadow Ant

Scientific name: *Lasius flavus*
Family: Formicidae

Appearance: Although you will seldom see this ant unless you specifically look for it, you will certainly see its nests, because these are the large mounds that can be so conspicuous in dry grasslands. The ants spend all their lives underground, 'milking' honeydew from subterranean aphids, which the ants herd like cattle. The nest in the illustration was under a flat stone, and several workers can be seen using their jaws to manipulate the fat sausage-like pupae.

Length: Females 8–9 mm; workers and males 3–5 mm.
Season: All year.
Where is it found? In dry grasslands, especially on chalk and limestone downlands.
Insect facts: In autumn the ants gather the large winter eggs laid by their 'pet' aphids, and incubate them in cells inside the nest. When spring arrives, the ants put the newly hatched aphids on the roots of their correct foodplants.

Red Ant

Scientific name: *Myrmica rubra*
Family: Formicidae

Appearance: This is the red ant most likely to be found just about anywhere in the British Isles, especially in gardens. The nest is placed under stones or logs. The winged males and females swarm in July and August. Like most ants, Red Ants tend and protect aphids, and 'milk' them for the sweet honeydew that they produce (*see* illustration).
Length: Females 5–7 mm; males and workers 4–5 mm.
Season: All year, hibernating in winter.
Where is it found? Just about everywhere.
Insect facts: Although Red Ants protect aphids, they attack and kill most other kinds of insects, including other ants.

Wood Ant

Scientific name: *Formica rufa*
Family: Formicidae

Appearance: This is our largest species of ant, with a black head and abdomen, and reddish thorax. Its large nests first draw attention because they consist of sizeable mounds of pine needles. Well-worn tracks lead out from the nests to the foraging grounds, which are usually trees laden with aphids.
Length: Male and queen 9–11 mm; worker 4–9 mm.
Season: Active March–November.
Where is it found? In pine and mixed woodlands.
Insect facts: When it is alarmed, a Wood Ant points the tip of its abdomen forwards, and squirts formic acid towards the enemy.

Slender-bodied Digger Wasp

Scientific name: *Crabro cribrarius*
Family: Sphecidae

Appearance: The males are peculiar in having the tibia of the front legs expanded, and shaped like a shovel. The legs of the female (illustrated) are quite strong and broad, and are heavily armed with conspicuous spines. In the similar Field Digger Wasp (*Mellinus arvensis*), which also catches flies, the legs are much more slender and less spiny. Our two other species of *Crabro* are much smaller than this one, although their males also have the expanded tibia on the front legs. Several species of *Ectemnius* look similar, and also catch flies, but nest in holes in rotting wood (including door frames and fence posts).
Length: 10–15 mm.
Season: May–August.
Where is it found? The Slender-bodied Digger often builds its nests in the ground in sandy places, such as heaths and sand-dunes, but it also excavates quite hard cliff-top paths, and even grassy banks in gardens. It occurs throughout the British Isles.
Insect facts: The female wasp catches large flies of many different families, such as bluebottles (illustrated), and airlifts them back to her nest. The flies then provide a source of fresh food for the wasp's larvae.

Sand-tailed Digger Wasp

Scientific name: *Cerceris arenaria*
Family: Sphecidae

Appearance: This wasp is generally similar to the previous species, but is rather slimmer, and the legs are almost entirely yellowish orange (the femora are almost entirely black in *Crabro cribrarius*). There is also a narrowing at the join between each abdominal segment, giving the abdomen an irregular, rather wavy edge instead of a smooth one. The nests often occur in hundreds on flat sandy ground.
Length: 13–16 mm.
Season: June–August.
Where is it found? In sandy places, as far north as Yorkshire.
Insect facts: The females of this wasp catch weevils, and take them back to the nest (illustrated). Each cell requires a stock of ten to fifteen weevils, to provide enough food for the larva within.

Great Sand Wasp

Scientific name: *Podalonia hirsuta*
Family: Sphecidae

Appearance: The body is much stockier than in the otherwise similar *Ammophila* spp, in which the abdomen is noticeably long and slender, with a very thin stalk at the front end. In *Podalonia* this stalk is stouter and shorter. In both genera the abdomen is orange, tipped black. The female wasp digs in sandy ground for hidden caterpillars, which she paralyses with a sting, and then drags to a suitable nesting area. She then digs a nest in the ground with her mandibles, hauls the caterpillar inside, and lays an egg on it. The caterpillar will provide fresh living food for the wasp's larva.

Length: 18–27 mm.
Season: May–October.
Where is it found? Mainly on coastal sand-dunes, but also on sandy heaths inland, as far north as Lancashire. It is absent from Ireland.

Leaden Spider Wasp

Scientific name: *Pompilus plumbeus*
Family: Pompilidae

Appearance: This active little wasp is entirely black, save for some pale greyish-blue bands on the abdomen, and a greyish-blue sheen to the legs. There are several other species with similar coloration. Several related species, which also catch spiders, have orange bands on the abdomen.
Length: 5–10 mm.
Season: May–August.
Where is it found? Mainly on coastal sand-dunes, particularly on the fore-dunes, where the sand is relatively unstable.
Insect facts: This wasp hunts wolf spiders, often attacking them face to face inside their own lairs.

Common Wasp

Scientific name: *Vespula vulgaris*
Family: Vespidae

Appearance: There are four species of similar-looking wasps in Britain, all of which are quite likely to be seen. Two of them, however, the Common Wasp and the German Wasp (*Vespula germanica*), are by far the most common. Unfortunately, all four are difficult to tell apart, unless you have detailed illustrations of their facial patterns. These wasps are likely to be seen scraping shavings from wooden fences and gates. The pulp is then used to make the paper that is used in nest building.

Length: Worker 12–15 mm; queen 17–19 mm.
Season: April–November.
Where is it found? Just about anywhere.
Insect facts: The Common Wasp builds its large paper nest under the ground, or in a rotting tree stump.

Hornet

Scientific name: *Vespa crabro*
Family: Vespidae

Appearance: This is the largest social wasp in Britain (or indeed in Europe), and it is a very handsome beast, with its elegant brown-and-yellow pattern (not black-and-yellow, as in other smaller wasps). The huge queens really are most impressive, especially when in flight. The nest is built inside a hollow tree or log, and in hot weather several workers will sit at the entrance, fanning cool air into the nest with their wings. This prevents the interior from overheating. Hornets can often be seen guzzling sap oozing from a wounded tree. They are not very aggressive – certainly less so than their smaller *Vespula* cousins.
Length: Worker 22–24 mm; queen 29–38 mm.
Season: March–October.
Where is it found? In southern and central areas of England and Wales; absent from Ireland.
Insect facts: Worker social wasps and ants are actually unmated females, that do not lay and rear any of their own eggs.

Tawny Mining Bee

Scientific name: *Andrena armata*
Family: Andrenidae

Appearance: With its black head, and dense coat of rusty brown hairs, the female of this bee (illustrated) cannot be mistaken for any other insect. The males are less often seen, and are smaller, slimmer, and mainly black with just a smattering of paler hairs.
Length: 10–12 mm.
Season: March–May.
Where is it found? Mostly in parks and gardens, over much of the British Isles.
Insect facts: The presence of Tawny Mining Bee nests on a lawn is betrayed by the little tell-tale piles of fine earth around each nest entrance, looking like tiny volcanoes.

Carder Bee

Scientific name: *Anthidium manicatum*
Family: Megachilidae

Appearance: This is a very chunky bee, with a squarish abdomen that has a row of yellow spots around the side and rear margins. The males are usually much bigger than the females, and can usually be seen hovering and darting around hairy leafed garden plants, such as Lamb's Tongue (*Stachys lanata*). The females come to this plant to scrape balls of fluff from the leaves, using this material to line their nests inside dead wood or walls.

Length: 8–15 mm.

Season: June–August.

Where is it found? In woodland rides, scrubby places, parks, and gardens, where it is often common.

Insect facts: The ball of fluff gathered by the female can be nearly as big as the bee herself.

Red Mason Bee

Scientific name: *Osmia rufa*
Family: Megachilidae

Appearance: This is rather like a slightly less furry version of the Tawny Mining Bee, which is a much brighter shade of red, and has far shorter antennae than the Red Mason Bee. In the illustration of a male courting a female, it can be seen that the male is much the smaller of the two.
Length: 10–15 mm.
Season: April–July.
Where is it found? Almost anywhere, but especially in gardens.
Insect facts: The Red Mason Bee often nests in holes in gates, fences, and wooden greenhouses. It will also excavate a nest in the soft mortar of old walls. It 'mines' mud from flowerbeds, using this material to build the partitions between the nest cells. When returning to the nest, it carries the blob of mud in its mouth.

Dune Snail Bee

Scientific name: *Osmia aurulenta*
Family: Megachilidae

Appearance: The females of this charming little bee are brown and quite hairy. The males are black and look like a different species. The easiest way to make a positive identification is to find the bee at its nest which is placed inside a disused snail shell.
Length: 10–12 mm.
Season: May–July.
Where is it found? On sand-dunes all around our coasts.
Insect facts: The female of this bee seals the opening in the snail shell with a curtain made of chewed-up leaves.

Large Garden Leaf-cutter Bee

Scientific name: *Megachile willughbiella*
Family: Megachilidae

Appearance: There are seven kinds of leaf-cutter bees in the British Isles, all of them looking much like this one. Pollen is collected on a brush of orange hairs beneath the abdomen, rather than on the hind legs. This bee is responsible for snipping semicircular and oval sections from the leaves of roses, beech hedges, and other garden plants. These leaf sections are used to make a sausage-shaped nest cell, usually within a cavity in timber.

Length: 12–15 mm.
Season: May–August.
Where is it found? Woodland rides and hedgerows, but also gardens, where it is especially common.
Insect facts: The Small Garden Leaf-cutter (*Megachile centuncularis*) is smaller (8–12 mm) and darker, but just as common in gardens.

Hairy-legged Mining Bee

Scientific name: *Dasypoda altercator*
Family: Megachilidae

Appearance: This fairly large brown bee can easily be identified by the dense mass of long hairs on the back legs; these are used for collecting copious quantities of pollen. It nests in dense aggregations on sandy paths and tracksides. It visits only flowers of the daisy family, and is especially fond of yellow hawkweeds.
Length: 13–15 mm.
Season: July–August.
Where is it found? Mainly on the coast, in sandy places.
Insect facts: The nest tunnel extends for up to 50 centimetres into quite hard ground – a feat of construction for a tiny insect using only its jaws and legs.

Yellow Nomad Bee

Scientific name: *Nomada flava*
Family: Anthophoridae

Appearance: There are more than twenty kinds of nomad bees in the British Isles, and several of them are similar to the species illustrated. Others are black and yellow, or black and white. They are all very wasp-like, and lack any hairs for collecting pollen. This is because they are parasites inside the nests of other solitary bees. The Yellow Nomad Bee targets *Andrena scotica* as its host.

Length: 10–12 mm.
Season: April–June.
Where is it found? In grassy places where the bee hosts nest.
Insect facts: Nomad bee females locate the nests of their hosts by smell.

Honey Bee

Scientific name: *Apis mellifera*
Family: Apidae

Appearance: The Honey Bee rather resembles some kinds of brown solitary bees, but is usually slightly larger and less hairy. The abdomen is often quite boldly striped in brownish orange, but it can also be almost uniformly dark brown. The bees that we normally see hurrying from flower to flower are workers, collecting nectar and pollen (note the mass of pollen on the hind leg of the bee illustrated) to take back to the colony. Most colonies are in hives, but many 'wild' colonies also occur in hollow trees.
Length: 10–15 mm.
Season: Active all summer long.
Where is it found? Anywhere with flowers.
Insect facts: Look for the fairly long antennae on any insect you suspect could be a Honey Bee. If the antennae are so short that they are scarcely visible, then it is an *Eristalis* sp Drone-fly (*see* illustration).

Small Garden Bumble-bee

Scientific name: *Bombus hortorum*
Family: Apidae

Appearance: There are two yellow bands on the thorax, one at the front and one at the rear, separated by a broad black area. The abdomen has a broad yellow band at the front, followed by a broad area of black, and finished off with a white tail.
Length: 10–22 mm.
Season: March–November.
Where is it found? Wherever there are flowers, especially in gardens.
Insect facts: Although it usually nests in the ground, the nests of this bee can sometimes be found in the open, covered by a small pile of grass.

White-tailed Bumble-bee

Scientific name: *Bombus lucorum*
Family: Apidae

Appearance: There is only a single yellow band on the thorax, forming a collar behind the head. In the middle of the abdomen there is a yellow band, equal in width to the black areas on either side, followed by a white tail. As in all bumble-bees, the queen (illustrated) is much bigger than the workers. The mated queens hibernate through the winter, and start a new colony in spring.
Length: 10–20 mm.
Season: February–November.
Where is it found? Wherever there are flowers.
Insect facts: The most common form of the Bumble-bee Fly (*Volucella bombylans*) looks very like this species and the preceding one. Look for the much longer, black antennae of the true bumble-bee.

Buff-tailed Bumble-bee

Scientific name: *Bombus terrestris*
Family: Apidae

Appearance: The yellow collar behind the head is narrower, and of a deeper gold than in the preceding species. The golden band on the abdomen is not in the middle, leaving a broader zone of black at the rear than in front (except in the male, in which the gold band is at the front). The tail is often buff, but can also be as white as in the preceding two species.
Length: 20–27 mm.
Season: March–October.
Where is it found? Very common in gardens and just about everywhere else.
Insect facts: This bumble-bee has quite a short tongue, so it often bites a hole at the base of certain flowers, to obtain the nectar.

Vestal Cuckoo Bumble-bee

Scientific name: *Bombus vestalis*
Family: Apidae

Appearance: This is very similar to the last species, in the nests of which it behaves as a 'cuckoo'. The absence of the yellow abdominal band in the Vestal Cuckoo Bumble-bee serves to distinguish it quite easily. The rear legs also lack the bright shiny pollen-baskets, found on the legs of ordinary bumble-bees.

Length: 20–27 mm.
Season: May–August.
Where is it found? In the same places as its host described above.
Insect facts: Cuckoo bumble-bees have a tough exterior and powerful sting, enabling them to bulldoze their way into their host's nest and take it over.

Early Bumble-bee

Scientific name: *Bombus pratorum*
Family: Apidae

Appearance: Male, queen, and worker each has a yellow collar behind the head, a narrow yellow band at the front of the abdomen, and a reddish tail.
Length: 10–22 mm.
Season: March–September.
Where is it found? In gardens and woodland rides.
Insect facts: Male bees are called drones and cannot sting.

Common Carder Bumble-bee

Scientific name: *Bombus pascuorum*
Family: Apidae

Appearance: This bee is easily recognized by its generally tawny coloration. The reddish-brown hair on the thorax is often fairly dense and, in the queen, the abdomen is almost equally densely clad but the workers usually have fairly bald, brownish-black abdomens. The Common Carder Bumble-bee always has a rather careworn appearance because the hairs are less dense than in other bumble-bees.
Length: 10–22 mm.
Season: April–November.
Where is it found? Common in most areas, especially in gardens.
Insect facts: The nest of this bee is always on or above the ground. The larval cells are covered in a mass of woven moss or grass.

Red-tailed Bumble-bee

Scientific name: *Bombus lapidarius*
Family: Apidae

Appearance: The workers and queens are inky black, save for bright-red tails. The male (illustrated) is similar, but has a brownish-yellow collar, and lacks the yellow abdominal band that is present in the very similar male of the Early Bumble-bee.

Length: 12–25 mm.
Season: April–August.
Where is it found? Just about anywhere.
Insect facts: This bee is mimicked by the red-tailed form of the Bumble-bee Fly (*Volucella bombylans*). Look for the fairly long black antennae in the genuine bee.

Spotted Caddisfly

Scientific name: *Limnephilus marmoratus*
Family: Limnephilidae

Appearance: Unlike most species of *Limnephilus*, which are brown, this species is greyish white, with black spots. At rest it sits with its long antennae pointed forwards, giving it some resemblance to a dead leaf. Although caddisflies are superficially moth-like, their wings are covered with hairs, not the scales found in moths and butterflies.
Length: 15 mm.
Season: July–August
Where is it found? By rivers and lakes.
Insect facts: Caddisfly larvae are mainly aquatic, and live inside little cases that they construct from bits of leaf, sticks, stones, or snail shells.

Buttercup Micro Moth

Scientific name: *Micropteryx calthella*
Family: Micropterigidae

Appearance: This is a tiny but rather pretty little moth, with burnished-golden wings. It is a very primitive member of the Lepidoptera, in that it has biting mouthparts for chewing up pollen, rather than a tubular proboscis for sipping nectar. It is often found in large numbers eating the pollen of Kingcup (*Caltha palustris*) and various yellow buttercups.
Wing span: 6 mm.
Season: May–June.
Where is it found? In damp meadows, marshes, and woodland rides, throughout the British Isles.
Insect facts: The caterpillar of this moth lives among damp soil and moss.

Gold-banded Long-horned Moth

Scientific name: *Nemophora degeerella*
Family: Incurvariidae

Appearance: This is one of a number of tiny moths with very long thread-like antennae. These are longer in the male (illustrated) than in the female, and indeed the male has the longest antennae of any British moth. The forewings are a metallic bronzy gold, with a transverse golden-yellow band.
Wing span: 6–8 mm.
Season: June–August.
Where is it found? In woodland.
Insect facts: The males of most long-horned moths form small swarms and perform aerial dances.

Brown Plume Moth

Scientific name: *Pterophorus monodactylus*
Family: Pterophoridae

Appearance: Plume moths are easily recognized by their very narrow forewings and plume-like hindwings, which are wrapped around the forewings when at rest. This is one of our commonest species. The White Plume Moth (*Pterophorus pentadactyla*) is similar, but is pure shining white.
Wing span: 24 mm.
Season: July–October.
Where is it found? Almost anywhere.
Insect facts: The adults overwinter among Ivy leaves and reappear in April.

Many-plumed Moth

Scientific name: *Alucita hexadactyla*
Family: Alucitidae

Appearance: Each of the four dark-brown wings is divided up into six slim plumes. No other British moth is at all similar. The adults hibernate during the winter and reappear in April or May.
Wing span: 12–14 mm.
Season: July–October.
Where is it found? In hedgerows, woodland rides, and gardens.
Insect facts: The caterpillars of this moth are pale pink, and eat the buds and flowers of honeysuckles.

Gold Swift Moth

Scientific name: *Hepialus hecta*
Family: Hepialidae

Appearance: Swift moths do not have a proboscis, so cannot feed as adults. The gold bands on the forewings are narrower in the male (illustrated) than in the female. The hindwings are a dull brown. As in all swift moths, the males perform a hovering flight over the ground.
Wing span: 30 mm.
Season: June–August.
Where is it found? Throughout the British Isles wherever bracken grows.
Insect facts: The caterpillars feed on the roots and stems of bracken.

Six-spot Burnet Moth

Scientific name: *Zygaena filipendulae*
Family: Zygaenidae

Appearance: Each bronzy black forewing bears six red spots, although one or more of these will sometimes coalesce. The Five-spot Burnet (*Zygaena trifolii*) is similar, but has only five red spots on each forewing. In both species the hindwings are red, with black margins. Burnet moths are active by day, and are much attracted to the flowers of knapweeds, thistles, and scabious. The black-and-yellow caterpillars feed on trefoils and vetches.
Wing span: 32–34 mm.
Season: July–August.
Where is it found? On downlands, heaths, cliff-tops, and in woodland rides, throughout the British Isles.
Insect facts: The bright colours of burnet moths, known as 'warning colours', advertise the fact that they are extremely poisonous to eat.

Common Forester Moth

Scientific name: *Adscita statices*
Family: Zygaenidae

Appearance: This is one of several similar-looking metallic-green species. The adults are found on flowers, especially vetches and Ragged Robin (*Lychnis flos-cuculi*).
Wing span: 22 mm.
Season: June–July.
Where is it found? In damp grassland, scattered throughout the British Isles.
Insect facts: The caterpillar feeds on Sorrel (*Rumex acetosa*).

Drinker Moth

Scientific name: *Philudoria potatoria*
Family: Lasiocampidae

Appearance: The adult moth is brown, but is very unlikely to be seen. The caterpillar (illustrated) can be quite conspicuous. It is bluish grey, with a longitudinal stripe consisting of numerous golden dots and dashes. There are two rows of tufts of shortish black hairs along the back. Along the lower body margins, overhanging the legs, there is a row of shaggy, downward-pointing, white hair tufts.
Caterpillar's length: 50–60 mm.
Season: The caterpillar is first seen from July to October, then again in April to June, after hibernating.
Where is it found? In damp, lush, grassy places such as marshes, woodland rides, and riverbanks, throughout the British Isles.
Insect facts: The common name comes from the caterpillar's habit of drinking water from grass, its usual foodplant.

Fox Moth

Scientific name: *Macrothylacia rubi*
Family: Lasiocampidae

Appearance: The adult moth is brown and seldom seen, although the males are on the wing by day and night. The caterpillar (illustrated) is often seen in autumn, when it is crawling around looking for somewhere to hibernate. It is velvety black, with orange bands between the segments, and densely hairy.
Caterpillar's length: 50–60 mm.
Season: The caterpillar is first seen in July, and is fully grown by October when it goes into hibernation. It emerges in March or April, and pupates without ever feeding again.
Where is it found? On heaths and moors, throughout the British Isles.
Insect facts: The caterpillar eats bramble, heathers, and other low-growing shrubs. It should not be handled, because the hairs can severely irritate the skin.

Lackey Moth

Scientific name: *Malacosoma neustria*
Family: Lasiocampidae

Appearance: The adult moth is pale brown, but is very rarely seen. By contrast, the caterpillars (illustrated) are very conspicuous and common. They are greyish blue, with a series of red, white, and black longitudinal stripes. There are two large, black, eye-like spots on the 'face'.
Caterpillar's length: 40–45 mm.
Season: Adult June–August; caterpillar May–June.

Where is it found? The Lackey Moth is common almost everywhere in the British Isles, although it is absent from Scotland. It is most abundant on the coast, but can be very common on fruit trees in gardens inland.
Insect facts: The young caterpillars live in communal roosts on silken webs that they spin on Blackthorn, Hawthorn, sallows, and other trees.

Emperor Moth

Scientific name: *Saturnia pavonia*
Family: Saturniidae

Appearance: With its large eye-like spots on all four wings, this big moth can be mistaken for no other. The males fly very rapidly during the day, following the odour-plume laid down by the females, which release a special scent designed to attract a mate from a long distance.
Wing span: 65–75 mm.
Season: April–May.
Where is it found? Throughout the British Isles, especially on heaths and moors, but also in largely agricultural areas.
Insect facts: The fully grown caterpillar is a handsome bright green, sparsely hairy, and has a row of black blotches and pink warts. It eats a wide variety of plants, but is most often found on heather and bramble.

Poplar Hawk Moth

Scientific name: *Laothoe populi*
Family: Sphingidae

Appearance: When at rest, this large moth closely resembles a dead and rather tattered brown leaf. This effect is enhanced by the manner in which the hindwings project in front of the forewings. There is a conspicuous reddish-brown patch at the base of the hindwings, although this is concealed beneath the forewings in the illustration.

Wing span: 75–80 mm.

Season: June–August.

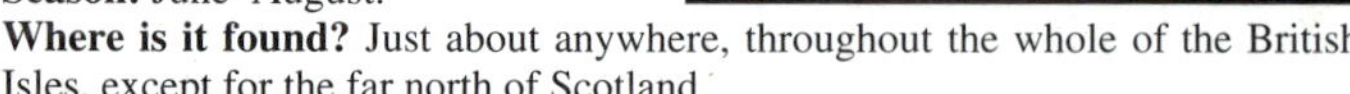

Where is it found? Just about anywhere, throughout the whole of the British Isles, except for the far north of Scotland.

Insect facts: The large caterpillar is green, with slanting yellow stripes along the sides, and a horn on the rear end. It feeds mainly on poplars and willows.

Elephant Hawk Moth

Scientific name: *Deilephila elpenor*
Family: Sphingidae

Appearance: The adult moth is similar to the next species, but is larger, with pink and yellow stripes on the forewings, and two broad yellow bands down either side of the bright-pink abdomen. The caterpillar (illustrated) can be either brown or green, and has two eye-like spots on either side, just behind its flexible trunk-like 'snout'. There is a short horn on the rear end. The caterpillar's main food is willowherbs.

Caterpillar's length: 50–60 mm.

Season: Adult May–July; caterpillar July–August.

Where is it found? Throughout the British Isles, except for northern Scotland, in virtually any habitat, including gardens.

Insect facts: When disturbed, the caterpillar pulls in its snout, so that the eye-spots swell up and are exposed at the front. It then sways from side to side like a miniature snake.

Small Elephant Hawk Moth

Scientific name: *Deilephila porcellus*
Family: Sphingidae

Appearance: The adult is much yellower than the mainly pink Elephant Hawk Moth (above), and can usually be found sitting low down among short grasses. Often several adults may be found in a small area. The caterpillar is brownish black, with two small, pink-centred, black eye-spots on either side, and no horn at the rear.
Wing span: 50 mm.
Season: June–July.
Where is it found? In dry grassy places, throughout the British Isles, except for the far north of Scotland.
Insect facts: The caterpillar feeds mainly on bedstraws (*Galium* spp).

Hummingbird Hawk Moth

Scientific name: *Macroglossum stellatarum*
Family: Sphingidae

Appearance: The forewings are brown, the hindwings mainly orange-yellow. There is a distinct tail tuft. This moth feeds during the day, and makes an audible hum as it hovers in front of flowers such as honeysuckle. It is a strong migrant, and mostly reaches our shores by crossing from mainland Europe.
Wing span: 40–45 mm.
Season: April–October.
Where is it found? Throughout the British Isles, although it is rare or absent in some years from many areas.
Insect facts: The caterpillar feeds on bedstraws (*Galium* spp) in July and August.

Puss Moth

Scientific name: *Cerura vinula*
Family: Notodontidae

Appearance: The adult moth is grey and white, but is very rarely seen. The caterpillar (illustrated) is well camouflaged on sallows and willows but well worth looking for because it is most interesting. It has a brown saddle on top and green sides, which are decorated with a row of black-margined white dots.
Length of caterpillar: 40–45 mm.
Season: Adult May–June; caterpillar July–August.
Where is it found? Throughout the British Isles, wherever sallows and willows grow.
Insect facts: When the caterpillar is alarmed, it rears its head up and lashes its whip-like 'tails' (modified back legs) to and fro. It also rears up its head to expose a rather intimidating-looking 'face'.

Buff-tip Moth

Scientific name: *Phalera bucephala*
Family: Notodontidae

Appearance: The adult moth is seldom seen. It has silvery forewings with a yellow patch at the tips, and a flat yellowish head. It looks rather like a small stick which has snapped off. At rest in daytime, it sits on leaves and not at the tips of broken sticks as is often incorrectly shown in books. In contrast to the retiring habits of the adults, the black-and-yellow, moderately hairy caterpillars form conspicuous masses on many garden trees.
Adults wingspan: 45–50 mm.
Season: Adult June–July; caterpillar July–September.
Where is it found? Just about anywhere, throughout the British Isles.
Insect facts: The caterpillars feed on almost any kind of tree or shrub.

Pebble Prominent Moth

Scientific name: *Eligmodonta ziczac*
Family: Notodontidae

Appearance: The adult moth is brown, but is seldom noticed unless it comes to a light. The caterpillar (illustrated) is more likely to be encountered. It is usually pale grey, but is often tinged with brown, pink, purple, or yellow. It has two humps in the middle, and another at the rear end which is normally curved upwards, away from the twig or leaf on which the caterpillar is sitting.

Length of caterpillar: 25 mm.

Season: Adult May–June; caterpillar July–September.

Where is it found? Throughout the British Isles, in marshes, fens, and damp woodland rides.

Insect facts: The caterpillar feeds on sallows, willows, and poplars.

Coxcomb Prominent Moth

Scientific name: *Ptilodon capucina*
Family: Notodontidae

Appearance: This moth is basically brown, with a prominent tuft of hairs on top of the thorax. The resemblance to a fallen dead leaf is marked, and this species is not easy to spot during daytime, even when a mating pair is exposed in full view on a leaf, as shown in the illustration.

Wing span: 42 mm.

Season: May–August.

Where is it found? Mainly in woodlands, throughout the British Isles.

Insect facts: The caterpillar is green, with a dark line down the middle of the back, and a yellow line along the sides. It feeds on various trees and shrubs.

Pale Prominent Moth

Scientific name: *Pterostoma palpina*
Family: Notodontidae

Appearance: The adult moth is greyish tan, streaked with black towards the wingtips. A tuft of black-tipped hairs protrudes above the back, between the folded wings, and long pale palps jut forward from the front end.
Wing span: 40–42 mm.
Season: May–August.
Where is it found? Almost anywhere throughout the British Isles, as far north as southern Scotland.
Insect facts: The caterpillar is bluish green, with white lines along the back and sides. Running through the spiracles (tiny breathing pores) is a yellow line, edged with black. The caterpillar occurs on poplars, willows, and sallows.

Pale Tussock Moth

Scientific name: *Callitaera pudibunda*
Family: Lymantriidae

Appearance: The adult moth is grey, but is very rarely noticed in nature. The caterpillar (illustrated) is much more conspicuous and attractive. It is green or lemon yellow, with a row of four broad, white, 'shaving-brush' hair tufts in the middle of its back, and a slimmer tuft of red hairs at the rear.

Length of caterpillar: 30 mm.
Season: Adult May–June; caterpillar July–September.
Where is it found? Everywhere, except for the far north of England and in Scotland.
Insect facts: The caterpillar eats the leaves of a wide variety of trees and other plants, including fruit trees in gardens.

Vapourer Moth

Scientific name: *Orgyia antiqua*
Family: Lymantriidae

Appearance: The brown male flies by day, but is seldom noticed. The female is wingless, and lays her eggs on her cocoon. The attractive caterpillar is frequently seen, as it often lives in gardens. The illustration serves to describe it, as there is nothing else similar.
Length of caterpillar: 30 mm.
Season: Adult May–August: caterpillar July–September.
Where is it found? Just about anywhere, throughout the British Isles.
Insect facts: The caterpillars feed on a wide variety of trees and shrubs, including several garden ornamentals.

Yellow-tail Moth

Scientific name: *Euproctis similis*
Family: Lymantriidae

Appearance: The white adult moth is rarely seen. When alarmed, it protrudes a yellowish-brown tail tuft up between its folded wings. The moderately hairy caterpillar is much more likely to be noticed. It is black, with a double red stripe down the middle of the back, and white splotches along the sides.
Wing span: 36 mm; length of caterpillar 32 mm.
Season: Adult July–August; caterpillar August–September, then going into hibernation, emerging in spring.
Where is it found? The Yellow-tail Moth is resident only in England and Wales but, within this region, it is widespread, especially in woodland rides, orchards, and gardens.
Insect facts: The caterpillar feeds on various trees, especially Hawthorn.

Garden Tiger Moth

Scientific name: *Arctia caja*
Family: Arctiidae

Appearance: This is quite a spectacular moth. The forewings are creamy white with brown blotches. The hindwings are bright reddish orange, with bluish-black ink spots. Although remarkably gaudy, the adult is rarely seen, because it conceals itself very well during the day.
Wing span: 38–40 mm.
Season: July–August.
Where is it found? Just about anywhere, but especially in towns, on roadsides, and in waste places, throughout the British Isles.
Insect facts: The very hairy, dark-brown caterpillar is known as the 'Woolly Bear'. It eats just about any low-growing garden plants, wild flowers, or weeds. It should not be touched because its hairs can cause severe irritation.

Scarlet Tiger Moth

Scientific name: *Callimorpha dominula*
Family: Arctiidae

Appearance: This spectacular moth is on the wing in daytime, when it often feeds at flowers. The forewings are black with white blotches, while the hindwings are bright red with black markings.
Wing span: 48 mm.
Season: June.
Where is it found? Locally, in fens, marshes, and damp woodland rides, over much of southern England and South Wales. The Scarlet Tiger is often abundant and conspicuous where it does occur.
Insect facts: The caterpillar is black, with a series of tiny yellow spots down the sides, more or less forming discrete bands. It feeds on a variety of plants, including nettles and Comfrey.

Cinnabar Moth

Scientific name: *Tyria jacobaeae*
Family: Arctiidae

Appearance: The adult moth has black forewings, with a red line down each front margin, and two red spots on the rear margins. The hindwings are red, with a narrow blackish border. The flight is usually very brief and fluttering. This species could easily be mistaken for a Burnet Moth, but the pattern is different.

Wing span: 28 mm.

Season: May–June.

Where is it found? In a variety of habitats, over the whole of the British Isles, except for northern Scotland.

Insect facts: The black-and-orange caterpillars form very conspicuous groups on *Senecio* spp ragwort plants.

Common Footman Moth

Scientific name: *Eilema lurideola*
Family: Arctiidae

Appearance: The adult moth has grey forewings, with a pale-yellowish margin that gradually narrows away towards the rear end (the margin is continued at its full width to the rear end in the similar Scarce Footman (*Eilema complana*). The hindwings are pale yellow [greyish yellow in the similar Dingy Footman (*Eilema griseola*)].
Wing span: 46 mm.
Season: July.
Where is it found? In woodlands over virtually the entire British Isles.
Insect facts: The grey hairy caterpillar of the Common Footman has black lines along its back, and an orange line on each side. It eats lichens growing on trees.

White Ermine Moth

Scientific name: *Spilosoma lubricipeda*
Family: Arctiidae

Appearance: The yellowish-white forewings bear scattered black spots, which vary somewhat in size, and may sometimes be absent. In some northern areas, specimens with buff forewings are not uncommon. The abdomen is yellowish orange, peppered with black spots. The very hairy caterpillar is brown, with an orange line down the middle of the back. It feeds on a wide variety of low-growing plants.
Wing span: 36 mm.
Season: May–July.
Where is it found? The White Ermine is common in most habitats, especially gardens, throughout the British Isles.

Grey Dagger Moth

Scientific name: *Apatele psi*
Family: Noctuidae

Appearance: The adult moth is grey, streaked with black, and sports a dark mark likened to the Greek letter 'psi', hence the scientific and common names. The adult is rarely seen, but the caterpillar can be quite common and conspicuous. It has a yellow band down the middle of the back, and a conspicuous pointed hair tuft on segment 4. Along each side there is a grey band, ornamented at regular intervals with red and black marks, like portholes. It feeds on all kinds of deciduous trees.
Length of caterpillar: 30–40 mm.
Season: Adult May–July; caterpillar August–October.
Where is it found? In most habitats throughout the British Isles. The caterpillars are often found on ornamental trees in gardens.

Broom Moth

Scientific name: *Ceramica pisi*
Family: Noctuidae

Appearance: The adult moth is basically brown, but is very rarely seen. In contrast, the long, smooth caterpillar (illustrated) is conspicuous and quite common, usually sitting in full view on its foodplant. Its main colour can be brown or green, with four bright-yellow stripes along the body.
Length of caterpillar: 40–45 mm.
Season: Adult June–July; caterpillar August–September.
Where is it found? In all kinds of habitats, throughout the British Isles.
Insect facts: The caterpillar feeds on a variety of plants from many different families, even including bracken, a fern shunned by many plant-eating insects.

The Coronet Moth

Scientific name: *Craniophora ligustri*
Family: Noctuidae

Appearance: The forewings are grey, heavily speckled with greenish or brownish. In the centre of each forewing there is a circular mark with a fanciful resemblance to a crown or coronet. The adult moths spend the day on tree trunks, where they are very difficult to spot.
Wing span: 20 mm.
Season: June–July.
Where is it found? In woods with ash trees, over most of the British Isles, but the Coronet is very rare in Ireland.
Insect facts: The caterpillar feeds in August and September on Ash (*Fraxinus excelsior*).

Mullein Moth

Scientific name: *Cucullia verbasci*
Family: Noctuidae

Appearance: The adult moth is straw coloured, with an upwardly projecting tuft of hairs behind its head, making it very twig- like, so it is seldom observed. The caterpillar (illustrated) is quite common and very conspicuous. It is smooth and white, with an abundance of black dots and yellow blotches, and a few black hairs.
Length of caterpillar: 40 mm.
Season: Adult April–May; caterpillar June–July.
Where is it found? Throughout England and Wales, often in waste places in towns.
Insect facts: The caterpillar usually eats Common Mullein (*Verbascum thapsus*), a typical plant of waste ground. It is also common on *Scrophularia* spp figworts, as illustrated.

Angle Shades Moth

Scientific name: *Phlogophora meticulosa*
Family: Noctuidae

Appearance: The adult moth bears a remarkable resemblance to a crinkled dead leaf. There are two large, brown, triangular marks on each forewing (although the brown on the forewings can sometimes be replaced by green). Often the whole moth is tinted a bright rosy red. It often chooses a resting place on the dead brown parts of plants, where it is very hard to spot, but it also frequently roosts on green leaves, as illustrated.

Wing span: 55 mm.

Season: May–October.

Where is it found? Almost everywhere, throughout the British Isles.

Insect facts: The smooth, green or brown caterpillar attacks just about any herbaceous plants. It can be a pest in gardens, especially on geraniums and chrysanthemums.

The Dun-bar Moth

Scientific name: *Cosmia trapezina*
Family: Noctuidae

Appearance: The ground colour of this moth is very variable, ranging from greyish buff to brick red. The cross-lines on the forewings enclose an area darker than the ground colour, sometimes even blackish. The moth may be found feeding on flowers in daytime, as illustrated.

Wing span: 25 mm.

Season: July–August.

Where is it found? In wooded country throughout the British Isles, except for northern Scotland.

Insect facts: The caterpillar feeds on the foliage of various trees, such as oak and sallow; it also eats other caterpillars, and is sometimes cannibalistic.

Burnished Brass Moth

Scientific name: *Diachrisia chrysitis*
Family: Noctuidae

Appearance: This common moth resembles a leaf which has recently died and fallen, but has not yet turned completely brown, so that a few green areas still remain. In the Scarce Burnished Brass (*Diachrisia chryson*), there is a single large greenish blotch on each forewing, rather than the two broad greenish bands of the Burnished Brass. The adult moth usually sits in full view on leaves, especially nettles, the caterpillar's foodplant.
Wing span: 36 mm.
Season: June–September.
Where is it found? Wherever nettles grow.

Herald Moth

Scientific name: *Scoliopteryx libatrix*
Family: Noctuidae

Appearance: This is another moth that resembles a dead leaf, although this time with a rather tattered rear margin. The basic colour is rusty brown, and there are two white spots on the forewings, the rear ends of which are crossed by two wavy white lines.
Wing span: 40 mm.
Season: August–October, then April–June after hibernation.
Where is it found? In gardens and woodlands throughout the British Isles.
Insect facts: The caterpillar is a long, slender, greenish beast, with little in the way of markings. It feeds on sallows and willows.

Silver Y Moth

Scientific name: *Autographa gamma*
Family: Noctuidae

Appearance: The ground colour of the wings is usually a dark blackish brown, and the Y-shaped mark, from which the common name is derived, is usually unbroken. In the Beautiful Golden Y (*Autographa pulchrina*) and Plain Golden Y (*Autographa jota*) the ground colour is a warm reddish brown, and the Y-shaped mark is usually broken in the middle. The Silver Y is commonly seen hovering in front of flowers as it feeds.
Wing span: 40 mm.
Season: May–November.
Where is it found? In all kinds of habitats throughout the British Isles, including gardens.
Insect facts: The caterpillar eats almost any kind of herbaceous vegetation.

Mother Shipton Moth

Scientific name: *Callistege mi*
Family: Noctuidae

Appearance: The markings on the forewings rather resemble a grotesque human mask, likened to the face of Mother Shipton, a legendary witch. This is one of our small band of day-flying moths, when it may be seen visiting wild flowers.

Wing span: 30 mm.
Season: May–June.
Where is it found? In all kinds of grassy places, such as chalk downs, railway embankments, and roadsides, but not in northern Scotland.
Insect facts: The caterpillar is brown, and feeds on clovers and melilots.

Silver-ground Carpet Moth

Scientific name: *Xanthorhoe montanata*
Family: Geometridae

Appearance: The ground colour of the adult moth is silvery white. There is a broad, brownish-black, wavy edged central band across each forewing. The adult sits in full view on low-growing plants, such as nettles, when it rather resembles a bird-dropping that has splashed on to the leaf.
Wing span: 30 mm.
Season: May–July.
Where is it found? In woodlands, lanesides, disused railway lines, etc., throughout the British Isles.
Insect facts: The caterpillar feeds on bedstraws and grasses.

Common Carpet Moth

Scientific name: *Epirrhoe alternata*
Family: Geometridae

Appearance: This moth is similar to the previous species, but is slightly smaller. The broad bands on the forewings can be either dark brown or greyish black, and a dark line always runs up the centre of the rearmost white band [this line is absent in the similar Wood Carpet (*Epirrhoe rivata*)].
Wing span: 24 mm.
Season: May–June, August–September.
Where is it found? Just about anywhere in the British Isles.
Insect facts: The caterpillar feeds on bedstraws.

Green Pug Moth

Scientific name: *Chloroclystis rectangulata*
Family: Geometridae

Appearance: The basic colour of this moth is grey or black, and the intensity of the green suffusion varies greatly, being more intense in freshly emerged individuals. The adult moths spend the day on algae-covered trees (the moth in the illustration was on a garden apple tree), when they are very difficult to spot.
Wing span: 23 mm.
Season: June–August.
Where is it found? In woods and gardens throughout the British Isles.
Insect facts: The caterpillar feeds on the flowers of Hawthorn, apples, and pears.

Magpie Moth

Scientific name: *Abraxas grossulariata*
Family: Geometridae

Appearance: The adult moth's pattern of black, white, and orange is so distinctive that it needs no further description. These colours serve a warning function, advertising to potential enemies, such as birds, that the moth has an unpleasant flavour.
Wing span: 44 mm.
Season: June–August.
Where is it found? The Magpie Moth is common in many places, most especially in gardens, throughout the British Isles.
Insect facts: The black-white-and-pink caterpillars are often seen in gardens, feeding on the leaves of gooseberries and currants.

Clouded Border Moth

Scientific name: *Lomaspilis marginata*
Family: Geometridae

Appearance: The shiny, bronzy black margins to the white wings make this attractive little moth quite unlike any other British species. The markings are rather variable, however, and not always as shown in the illustration. This is another moth that sits in full view and mimics a bird-dropping.
Wing span: 28 mm.
Season: May–August.
Where is it found? In woodlands, and along shady lanesides and riverbanks, throughout the whole of the British Isles, except for far northern Scotland.

Speckled Yellow Moth

Scientific name: *Pseudopanthera marginata*
Family: Geometridae

Appearance: This is another unmistakable moth, with its yellow wings heavily dotted with deep golden-brown, rather metallic speckles. It is on the wing during the day and, if disturbed, seldom flies far before fluttering down into the grass again.
Wing span: 27 mm.
Season: May–June.
Where is it found? In open woodland and on scrubby downland, throughout more or less the whole country.
Insect facts: The green caterpillar is embellished with white lines and stripes, and feeds on Wood Sage (*Teucrium scorodonium*), Hedge Woundwort (*Stachys sylvatica*), and dead nettle (*Lamium* spp).

Brimstone Moth

Scientific name: *Opisthograptis luteolata*
Family: Geometridae

Appearance: The leading edges of the pale-yellow forewings are marked with four brown blotches. Each forewing also bears a black-edged, white mark, resembling the silhouette of a bird in flight.
Wing span: 32 mm.
Season: April–October.
Where is it found? In all kinds of habitats, throughout the country.
Insect facts: The twig-like caterpillar mainly feeds on Hawthorn, but also occurs on Plum and Sloe.

Peppered Moth

Scientific name: *Biston betularia*
Family: Geometridae

Appearance: The adult moth is white, speckled with greyish black; a black form also occurs in towns. It spends the day on tree trunks, and is very seldom seen. The green, brown, or grey caterpillar (illustrated) is often found in gardens. It is a remarkable mimic of a twig, and can be very hard to spot. The head is deeply notched. It eats the leaves of a huge variety of trees and shrubs.
Length of caterpillar: 30 mm.
Season: Adult May–August; caterpillar June–September.
Where is it found? In all kinds of habitats throughout the British Isles. It is quite common in gardens.
Insect facts: The caterpillars of geometrid moths are called loopers or inchworms, because of their method of moving. With the front legs grasping a twig, the rear claspers are brought forwards to meet them, thereby forming the body into a loop above. The caterpillar then releases its hold with its front legs, stretches forwards a full body length, and grasps the twig with its front legs. It then again brings the hind claspers to meet the front legs, and so on.

Common Heath Moth

Scientific name: *Ematurga atomaria*
Family: Geometridae

Appearance: In the female (illustrated) the ground colour of the wings is white, fairly heavily speckled with dark bronzy brown. In the male the brown speckling is even denser, so that it almost obscures the yellow ground colour. The adult moth is on the wing in daytime.
Wing span: 24 mm.
Season: May–September.
Where is it found? On heaths and moors throughout the British Isles.
Insect facts: The caterpillar feeds mainly on heather.

Mottled Beauty Moth

Scientific name: *Alcis repandata*
Family: Geometridae

Appearance: The adult is usually silvery black, but some forms are dark brown, sparingly marked with dark wavy lines and faint mottling. During the day, this moth rests on tree trunks, as illustrated, with the wings aligned vertically up and down the trunk.

Wing span: 44 mm.
Season: June–July.
Where is it found? In woodlands, gardens, and orchards, throughout the British Isles.
Insect facts: The caterpillar feeds on many different plants, including heathers, Bilberry, birch, and Hawthorn.

Small White Butterfly

Scientific name: *Artogeia rapae*
Family: Pieridae

Appearance: The male butterfly depicted in the illustration is from the first brood in springtime. In this early form, the clouding on the tips of the forewings is only faint, and so is the single black spot (sometimes absent) on each forewing. In the later, summer brood the black is much darker. The female has two black spots on each forewing.
Wing span: 42 mm.
Season: April–October.
Where is it found? In open countryside, agricultural land, and gardens, throughout the British Isles.
Insect facts: The caterpillar is green, sprinkled with black. It has a yellowish line down the middle of the back, and a line consisting of yellow spots along the sides. It feeds on any plants of the cabbage family.

Green-veined White Butterfly

Scientific name: *Artogeia napi*
Family: Pieridae

Appearance: Even when it is feeding on flowers, this butterfly normally keeps its wings fully or partially closed, permitting a close view of the undersides. These bear a network of conspicuous greenish-black veins, more prominent on the hindwings than on the forewings, and quite unlike any other British butterfly.

Wing span: 43 mm.

Season: April–October.

Where is it found? Mainly in woodlands and marshes, over the whole of the British Isles, except for the far north of Scotland.

Insect facts: The caterpillar is similar to that of the Small White, and eats the same range of plants.

Large White Butterfly

Scientific name: *Pieris brassicae*
Family: Pieridae

Appearance: The two black spots on the forewing are restricted to the female (illustrated). The undersides of all four wings are often white, but the hindwing can also be heavily dusted with yellow. In the spring brood (illustrated), the black markings are less intense than in the summer brood.
Wing span: 50 mm.
Season: May–October.
Where is it found? Throughout the British Isles, in most kinds of habitats.
Insect facts: The caterpillar is yellow, heavily dotted with black. It eats most plants of the cabbage family, and can be a pest in gardens.

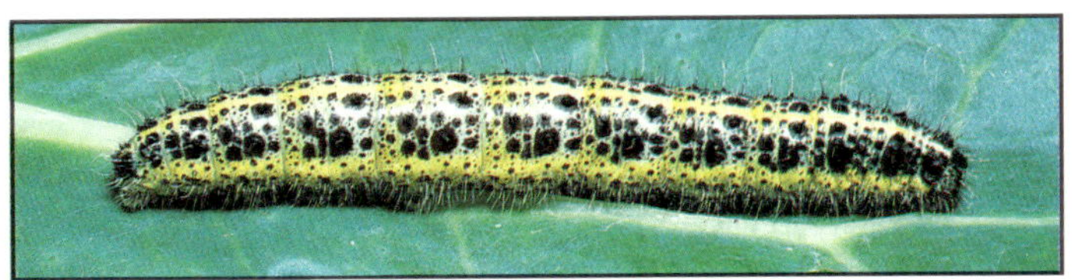

Orange-tip Butterfly

Scientific name: *Anthocharis cardamines*
Family: Pieridae

Appearance: Only the male (illustrated) has the prominent orange patches on the tips of the forewings. In the female, these patches are smaller and black. The undersides of the hindwings are heavily marked with a pattern of tiny black and yellow dots. From a distance this pattern gives the impression of being green.
Wing span: 40 mm.
Season: April–June.
Where is it found? On roadsides, disused railway lines, in marshes, and along woodland rides, throughout the British Isles, except for northern Scotland.
Insect facts: The green caterpillar feeds mainly on Lady's Smock (*Cardamine pratensis*) and Garlic Mustard (*Alliaria petiolata*). It is well camouflaged and very hard to spot.

Clouded Yellow Butterfly

Scientific name: *Colias croceus*
Family: Pieridae

Appearance: The male (illustrated) is a deep bright yellow. Most females are similar, but some are a very pale shade of greenish white. The Clouded Yellow reaches our shores as a migrant, and is unable to survive our harsh winters. In some years, large numbers arrive from continental Europe, and reach all parts of Britain. In other years arrivals are scarce.
Wing span: 44 mm.
Season: Mostly in August, but some immigrants arrive April–May and breed here.
Insect facts: The caterpillar feeds on clovers and related plants.

Brimstone Butterfly

Scientific name: *Gonepteryx rhamni*
Family: Pieridae

Appearance: The male (illustrated) is a bright lemon yellow. The female is greenish white. The males spend much of their time flying up and down, searching for females perched on vegetation. This is not an easy task, as a female at rest closely resembles a pale dead leaf. Both sexes often feed at flowers, especially thistles.
Wing span: 48 mm.
Season: July–September, and then April–May, after hibernation.
Where is it found? In most habitats, throughout the British Isles, except for the northern regions of Scotland and Ireland.
Insect facts: The green caterpillar feeds on buckthorns.

Peacock Butterfly

Scientific name: *Inachis io*
Family: Nymphalidae

Appearance: This is the only British butterfly with four prominent eye-spots on the wings, so it cannot be mistaken for any other species (except perhaps the Emperor Moth, which is grey). The undersides of the wings are blackish, and, when at rest, the Peacock looks reasonably like a dead leaf. The male and female are identical.
Wing span: 58 mm.
Season: July–October, and then again March–June, after hibernation.
Where is it found? In most habitats, throughout the British Isles, except for the far north of Scotland. The Peacock is particularly common in gardens.
Insect facts: The velvety black caterpillars are peppered with white dots, and feed communally on Stinging Nettles.

Comma Butterfly

Scientific name: *Polygonia c-album*
Family: Nymphalidae

Appearance: With its ragged-edged wings, the Comma is like no other British butterfly. The uppersides of the wings are a warm brownish orange, with black spots. The undersides are brown, often variegated with a greenish pattern, and always bearing a conspicuous white, comma-shaped mark. At rest, with its wings closed, the Comma resembles a dead oak leaf.
Wing span: 46 mm.
Season: There is a lighter-brown summer generation that flies July–August. A darker-brown autumn generation is on the wing August–October, and then again March–May after hibernation.
Where is it found? In many different habitats in south and central England.
Insect facts: The brown-and-white spiky caterpillars feed mainly on nettle, currant, hop, and gooseberry.

Painted Lady Butterfly

Scientific name: *Vanessa cardui*
Family: Nymphalidae

Appearance: The uppersides of the wings are a mixture of pale orange, black, and white. No other British butterfly is similar. The Painted Lady is a great migrant, and, in some years (such as 1996), huge numbers of butterflies reach our shores in springtime from Europe or North Africa. These immigrants make their way inland, laying eggs as they go, so that later in the summer there is a British-bred generation. There is no return migration, and the locally bred butterflies die with the onset of winter.
Wing span: 56 mm.
Season: April–May, July–October.
Where is it found? In good years the Painted Lady is distributed throughout the British Isles, but in poor years it reaches only the south.
Insect facts: The large, spiky grey caterpillar lives inside a silken web on thistles.

Red Admiral Butterfly

Scientific name: *Vanessa atalanta*
Family: Nymphalidae

Appearance: The uppersides of the wings are a deep velvety black, with four broad red bands, and a series of white blotches on the tips of the forewings. Adults seen in springtime are probably early migrants from southern Europe or North Africa. These lay eggs, resulting in a locally bred generation later in the summer. Red Admirals are often found on flowers, especially garden Buddliea, but they may also be found in some numbers sipping the juice oozing from fallen plums or apples.
Wing span: 60 mm.
Season: April–May, July–October.
Where is it found? In most kinds of habitat throughout the British Isles.
Insect facts: The caterpillars feed singly on nettles.

Small Tortoiseshell Butterfly

Scientific name: *Aglais urticae*
Family: Nymphalidae

Appearance: The uppersides of the wings are an attractive combination of orange and black, with a series of blue marks along the margins. The Small Tortoiseshell is particularly attracted to garden flowers, such as Buddliea and Ice Plant [*Sedum spectabile* (illustrated)] on which it may throng in some numbers.
Wing span: 50 mm.
Season: There is an early brood in June, followed by a summer brood August–October. The adults then go into hibernation and emerge again in early spring to lay eggs.
Where is it found? In all kinds of habitats throughout the British Isles.
Insect facts: The spiky caterpillars are yellowish, speckled with black, and feed communally on nettles.

Small Pearl-bordered Fritillary

Scientific name: *Clossiana selene*
Family: Nymphalidae

Appearance: As in all our fritillaries, this butterfly is a rich brownish orange, spotted with black. The Pearl-bordered Fritillary (*Clossiana euphrosyne*) is similar but larger (wing span 45 mm), and has a large silver spot in the middle of a broad yellow band that runs through the middle of the underside of each hindwing. This spot is absent in the Small Pearl-bordered Fritillary.

Wing span: 42 mm.
Season: May–July.
Where is it found? In woodland rides and on heaths, throughout mainland Britain, but not in Ireland.
Insect facts: The black caterpillar feeds on violets, and hibernates through the winter when still very small.

Dark Green Fritillary

Scientific name: *Mesoacidalia aglaja*
Family: Nymphalidae

Appearance: This is a much bigger butterfly than the previous species, and there is a white hind margin to the wings. The undersides of the hindwings are extensively suffused with green, and bear several large silver spots. The Dark Green Fritillary is a very fast flier, and a brief glimpse as it dashes past is often the only contact with this splendid species.
Wing span: 54 mm.
Season: July–August.
Where is it found? In rough, grassy places such as downlands, heaths, moors, cliff-tops and sand-dunes, throughout the British Isles.
Insect facts: The caterpillar feeds on violets.

Marbled White Butterfly

Scientific name: *Melanargia galathea*
Family: Nymphalidae

Appearance: This is the only black-and-white butterfly in the British Isles, so it is unmistakable. The caterpillars eat various grasses. The adults are particularly fond of knapweed flowers, and form communal roosts among long grasses in the evening.

Wing span: 46 mm.

Season: June–August.

Where is it found? Rather locally in dry grassland, mainly on chalk and limestone downland, and sand-dunes, but sometimes common on railway embankments. The Marbled White is almost restricted to southern England, and even there it is commonest in the east.

Insect facts: The Marbled White and the following seven species are often included in their own family, the Satyridae.

Grayling Butterfly

Scientific name: *Hipparchia semele*
Family: Nymphalidae

Appearance: The upperside is a brownish orange but is seldom seen because the Grayling keeps its wings closed most of the time. The undersides are marked with various shades of grey, making the butterfly very hard to spot when it is basking on open ground, which is something it does most of the time.
Wing span: 48 mm.
Season: July–August.
Where is it found? In open habitats such as heaths, moors, hilltops, and sand-dunes, throughout the British Isles.
Insect facts: When it basks on the ground, the Grayling tilts its body over to one side.

Ringlet Butterfly

Scientific name: *Aphantopus hyperantus*
Family: Nymphalidae

Appearance: The upperside is dark sooty brown, marked in the female with several white-centred black spots. These are usually absent in the even darker male. The undersides are pale brown, and bear a series of small eye-like black spots, with white centres and yellow margins.
Wing span: 40 mm.
Season: July–August.
Where is it found? On woodland edges, lanesides, riverbanks, and along old railway lines, throughout the British Isles, except for the northern half of Scotland.
Insect facts: The brown caterpillar eats grass.

Gatekeeper Butterfly

Scientific name: *Pyronia tithonus*
Family: Nymphalidae

Appearance: This butterfly is vaguely similar to the Meadow Brown (*see* below), but the Gatekeeper is smaller and has much larger orange patches on the wings. On each forewing there is a black spot, usually containing two white dots, although one or both of these can be absent in the male.

Wing span: 38–40 mm.
Season: June–August.
Where is it found? Along hedgerows, woodland edges, country lanesides, and old railway lines. The Gatekeeper occurs throughout all of England and Wales, but is absent from Scotland and the northern two-thirds of Ireland.
Insect facts: It is thought that this brown butterfly gets its name from its habit of settling on gate-posts.

Meadow Brown Butterfly

Scientific name: *Maniola jurtina*
Family: Nymphalidae

Appearance: In the male (illustrated) the orange patch on each forewing is relatively small, and the black spot has a single white pupil. In females the orange is more extensive, and the black spot usually has two white pupils.
Wing span: 46 mm.
Season: June–September.
Where is it found? In any areas of wild, uncultivated grass, throughout the British Isles; our commonest butterfly.

Small Heath Butterfly

Scientific name: *Coenonympha pamphilus*
Family: Nymphalidae

Appearance: The upperside is plain brownish orange, but is seldom seen, because the Small Heath almost always keeps its wings closed, even when feeding at flowers. The Large Heath (*Coenonympha tullia*) is much larger (wing span 36 mm), and has several conspicuous black eye-spots on the undersides.
Wing span: 28 mm.
Season: July–August.
Where is it found? Usually resting among grass in rough, grassy places, especially on moors, heaths, and downlands, throughout the British Isles.

Speckled Wood Butterfly

Scientific name: *Pararge aegeria*
Family: Nymphalidae

Appearance: The ground colour of the wings is dark brown. There is a single, white-centred black spot near the tip of each forewing, and three similar spots towards the rear of the hindwings. This butterfly is usually seen resting on leaves, with its wings spread, but it is also found on a variety of flowers. It is especially fond of sipping the juice oozing from ripe blackberries.
Wing span: 42 mm.
Season: April–October.
Where is it found? On woodland edges and in other shady places, including gardens; all over, except for northern Scotland.

Wall Brown Butterfly

Scientific name: *Lasiommata megera*
Family: Nymphalidae

Appearance: This butterfly is a bright brownish orange, with a pattern of dark lines. There is a lone, white-centred black spot near the front of each forewing, and four more – two large and two small – near the margin of each hindwing. The female is slightly larger than the male, which has a broad, blackish sexual brand on the central area of his forewings. The Wall Brown spends much of its time basking on walls, fences, gates, and large stones.

Wing span: 44–46 mm.
Season: May–August.
Where is it found? On woodland edges, lanesides, and dry banks, throughout the British Isles, except for most of Scotland.

Green Hairstreak Butterfly

Scientific name: *Callophrys rubi*
Family: Lycaenidae

Appearance: The upperside of this little butterfly is brown but is seldom seen because it normally keeps its wings shut, except when in flight. The underside is a lovely bright green, with a streak of fine white dots across the rear sector of each hindwing. No other British butterfly is similar.
Wing span: 29 mm.
Season: May–June.
Where is it found? On woodland margins, scrubby downlands, heaths, and moors, throughout the British Isles.
Insect facts: The squat green caterpillar feeds on a variety of plants, including broom and gorse.

Small Copper Butterfly

Scientific name: *Lycaena phlaeas*
Family: Lycaenidae

Appearance: The forewings are a bright coppery orange, spotted with black, and with black outer margins. The hindwings are black, with an orange band along the outer margins. Some specimens are blacker than the one illustrated.
Wing span: 29 mm.
Season: May–October.
Where is it found? In every kind of habitat, including gardens, throughout the British Isles, except for northern Scotland.
Insect facts: The stumpy green caterpillar feeds on docks and sorrel.

Common Blue Butterfly

Scientific name: *Polyommatus icarus*
Family: Lycaenidae

Appearance: The male's upperside (illustrated) is blue, patterned with black veins that terminate at the white wing margins. In the similar, but rarer, Adonis Blue (*Lysandra bellargus*), the black veins continue through the white border right to the wing edges. In both species the females are brown, with some blue towards the wing-bases. This blue is often quite extensive in some female Common Blues, which almost resemble males.
Wing span: 24 mm.
Season: May–September.
Where is it found? In open grassland, woodland rides, and any places with short grass and the necessary larval foodplants, even on roadside verges in large towns; throughout the British Isles.
Insect facts: The caterpillar feeds mainly on Bird's-foot Trefoil (*Lotus corniculatus*).

Chalkhill Blue Butterfly

Scientific name: *Lysandra coridon*
Family: Lycaenidae

Appearance: The male (illustrated) is of a paler and much more silvery blue than the male of the Common Blue. There is a fairly broad, blackish border to the wings, fringed with white. The female is a rather drab brown, tinted with blue to varying degrees, and quite extensively blue in some individuals. The Chalkhill Blue is a noticeably larger butterfly than either the Common or Adonis Blues. This size difference is quite important in localities where all three species occur together.
Wing span: 38 mm.
Season: July–August.
Where is it found? On chalk and limestone downland in southern and south-central England.

Holly Blue Butterfly

Scientific name: *Celastrina argiolus*
Family: Lycaenidae

Appearance: The upperside of this butterfly is bright blue in the male, and blue with broad brown margins in the female. Unlike other 'blues', however, the Holly Blue tends to keep its wings closed most of the time. The undersides are silvery, with a few tiny black spots, and therefore rather similar to the Small Blue (*Cupido minimus*). The latter is easily identified, however, by its small size (wing span only 22 mm) and brown uppersides. The other 'blues' all have much prettier undersides, which are heavily spotted with black and orange.

Wing span: 30 mm.
Season: In two broods, April–May and July–August.
Where is it found? In many kinds of habitats, including gardens, everywhere except the most northerly parts of England and the whole of Scotland.
Insect facts: Females of the first brood lay their eggs on Holly, Dogwood, and Buckthorn. The second brood develops on Ivy.

Brown Argus Butterfly

Scientific name: *Aricia agestis*
Family: Lycaenidae

Appearance:. Both male and female have brown uppersides. There is a row of bright-orange spots near the margins of all four wings. The caterpillar feeds on Rockrose (*Helianthemum nummularium*).

Wing span: 30 mm.

Season: May–June, and then again in August.

Where is it found? On chalk and limestone grassland, heaths, and moors, over south and central England and the whole of Wales, but not in northern England, Scotland, or Ireland.

Small Skipper Butterfly

Scientific name: *Thymelicus sylvestris*
Family: Hesperiidae

Appearance: The tops of the wings are a uniform brownish orange, with a black sexual brand in the male. As in most skippers, the wings are normally held in the manner seen in the illustration, except when the butterfly is in the shade, sleeping, or mating, when the wings are held vertically above the back.
Wing span: 28 mm.
Season: July–August.
Where is it found? In grassy places, woodland rides, cliff-tops, etc., over the southern half of England and Wales.

Large Skipper Butterfly

Scientific name: *Ochlodes venatus*
Family: Hesperiidae

Appearance: The brown of the wings is less orange than in the Small Skipper, and is marked with pale blotches. The underside is paler and mostly unmarked, or sometimes with some faint pale spots. The upperside of the Silver-spotted Skipper (*Hesperia comma*) is similar but, in this attractive species, there is a strong green tinge on the underside, along with several large silvery spots.
Wing span: 30 mm.
Season: June–August.
Where is it found? In grassy places as far north as southern Scotland, but not in Ireland.

Dingy Skipper Butterfly

Scientific name: *Erynnis tages*
Family: Hesperiidae

Appearance: This smallish brown butterfly could easily be mistaken for a moth, so it is important to inspect its pattern carefully in the illustration. It does not hold its wings in the special manner seen in the previous two skippers, but spreads them out to the sides, as in other butterflies. The rather similar Grizzled Skipper (*Pyrgus malvae*) is smaller, blackish grey, and heavily spotted with cream dots.
Wing span: 28 mm.
Season: May–June.
Where is it found? Mainly on chalk and limestone downlands, over much of the country, but very rare in the north and in Ireland.

Common Scorpionfly

Scientific name: *Panorpa communis*
Family: Panorpidae

Appearance: The male Scorpionfly (illustrated), with his upturned, scorpion-like, tail-mounted genital capsule (which is absent in the female), is unlike any other British insect. Note the long snout and the spotted wings. In the German Scorpionfly (*Panorpa germanica*) the black spots are more scattered.
Wing span: 24–30 mm.
Season: May–August.
Where is it found? In damp shady places, over most of the country.
Insect facts: Scorpionflies are scavengers, feeding on insects that are already dead. They often enter spiders' webs to feed on prey that the spider has temporarily deserted.

Spotted Crane Fly

Scientific name: *Nephrotoma appendiculata*
Family: Tipulidae

Appearance: The female's long, slender, yellow abdomen ends in a point, and bears three longitudinal black stripes. In the male (lowermost of this mating pair) the abdomen is more blunt ended and blacker. In both sexes, the thorax is yellow, spotted with black. As in all crane flies, the legs are long and thread-like.
Length: 16–18 mm.
Season: May–August.
Where is it found? Throughout the British Isles, in most kinds of habitats, including gardens.

Small Yellow Crane Fly

Scientific name: *Limnophila ferruginea*
Family: Tipulidae

Appearance: This is one of our more attractive crane flies, with its bright-yellow abdomen, adorned with a row of black spots. The illustration depicts a female, which can be easily recognized by her red-tipped, pointed abdomen. The male's abdomen is blunt ended and distinctly swollen towards the tip.
Length: 10 mm.
Season: June–September.
Where is it found? In damp places, such as marshes and gravel pits, over much of the British Isles.

False Crane Fly

Scientific name: *Ptychoptera contaminata*
Family: Ptychopteridae

Appearance: The black legs of this species are noticeably stouter than in any true crane flies (Tipulidae). The body is black, with a few brown markings. In the female the wings are more or less clear but, in the male, they are spotted with black. The adults are usually seen sitting around on waterside vegetation.
Length: 12–14 mm.
Season: May–October.
Where is it found? Beside ponds, lakes, and slow-moving rivers, throughout the British Isles.
Insect facts: The larva lives in fresh water and has a long 'tail' which functions as a breathing tube.

Ring-legged Mosquito

Scientific name: *Culiseta annulata*
Family: Culicidae

Appearance: This is one of the largest British mosquitoes. It may be easily recognized by the broad whitish rings on the legs, the silver bands on the abdomen, and the spotting on the wings. The males are distinguished by their feathery antennae, and their lack of blood-sucking habits. In the illustration two males are holding on to a female. The eggs are laid in miniature rafts on stagnant water.
Length: 7 mm.
Season: May–July.
Where is it found? By shaded stagnant water; the females often hibernate inside houses.
Insect facts: Mosquito larvae move around in water by making repeated vigorous jerks of the body. They have to come to the surface to breath air, using a siphon at the tip of the abdomen.

Non-biting Midge

Scientific name: *Chironomus plumosus*
Family: Chironomidae

Appearance: Non-biting Midges often occur in huge swarms of millions over and beside lakes and ponds. The wings are shorter than the body (the wings are longer than the body in mosquitoes) and are held roof-like above the body when not in use. Only the male (illustrated) has feathery (plumose) antennae. Some species of non-biting midges are a beautiful shade of bright green.

Length: 7 mm.
Season: April–September.
Where is it found? Common everywhere by lakes and ponds.
Insect facts: The aquatic larvae of these midges are called bloodworms, because of their red coloration. Their blood contains the red pigment haemoglobin (which is present in human blood), a relatively rare occurrence in insects.

Common St Mark's Fly

Scientific name: *Bibio marci*
Family: Bibionidae

Appearance: As a group, St Mark's flies are slim-bodied, usually black, hairy flies that swarm in huge numbers over grasslands. This very common species is usually on the wing on St Mark's Day (25 April), hence its common name. The males have very large eyes which meet on top of the head, and they trail their legs down behind them when hovering in their large mating swarms. The female (on the left in this mating pair) has normal eyes, and a much more pointed head.
Length: 8–10 mm.
Season: April–May.
Where is it found? In meadows throughout the British Isles.
Insect facts: There are several more similar-looking black species, while others are brown or have brown legs.

Hairy-eyed Soldier Fly

Scientific name: *Chloromyia formosa*
Family: Stratiomyidae

Appearance: Most soldier flies have flattened bodies and fold their wings flat over the body when at rest, concealing the bright colours typical of the group. This species holds its wings out at the sides, exposing the dark metallic-green thorax and reddish-brown metallic abdomen. The eyes are densely hairy.
Length: 8 mm.
Season: May–July.
Where is it found? In all kinds of habitats, including gardens, throughout the British Isles.

Down-looker Fly

Scientific name: *Rhagio scolopaceus*
Family: Rhagionidae

Appearance: The top of the grey thorax bears two pale stripes, while the brown abdomen is heavily blotched with black. The wings are sparingly patterned with cloudy spots. This fly's common name comes from its habit of spending almost its entire adult life sitting, head downwards, on tree trunks. Several other common members of the genus look similar, but sit in a normal fashion on vegetation, and lack any cloudy spotting on the wings.
Length: 12–14 mm.
Season: May–August.
Where is it found? In most habitats, but especially in woodlands, throughout the British Isles.
Insect facts: The carnivorous larva lives in the ground.

Golden Snipe Fly

Scientific name: *Chrysopilus cristatus*
Family: Rhagionidae

Appearance: Fresh specimens are clothed in a dense pile of beautiful golden hairs and scales, although these soon begin to rub off. The male (on the right in the illustration of mating pair) is much slimmer than the female, and his eyes are very large, meeting on top of the head, which is therefore wider than the abdomen. The legs are long, and the body curves downwards towards the rear end.

Length: 7–8 mm.

Season: May–August.

Where is it found? In damp woodland rides, wooded marshes, and on riverbanks, throughout the British Isles.

Insect facts: The larvae develop in damp, rotting wood and leaf mould.

Giant Horse Fly

Scientific name: *Tabanus bovinus*
Family: Tabanidae

Appearance: This is one of our largest flies, and the pain of its bite will soon announce its presence, even if you fail to hear the hum of its arrival. The abdomen is much browner than in the closely similar *Tabanus sudeticus* which has a much darker and blacker appearance.
Length: 19–24 mm.
Season: July–August.
Where is it found? In woods, marshes, and pastures, throughout the British Isles.
Insect facts: The males do not bite and have large eyes that meet on top of the head. The female (illustrated) has normal eyes.

Cleg Fly

Scientific name: *Haematopota pluvialis*
Family: Tabanidae

Appearance: This is by far the commonest horsefly in most areas, and the one most likely to trouble you while on a country walk. The heavily spotted wings are held roof-like above the body, and the hairy eyes shine with a shifting pattern of iridescent blue and red. The Cleg Fly's flight is silent, and it is very persistent in its attentions, which is why it is such a nuisance. Several other species are very similar but are generally much rarer.

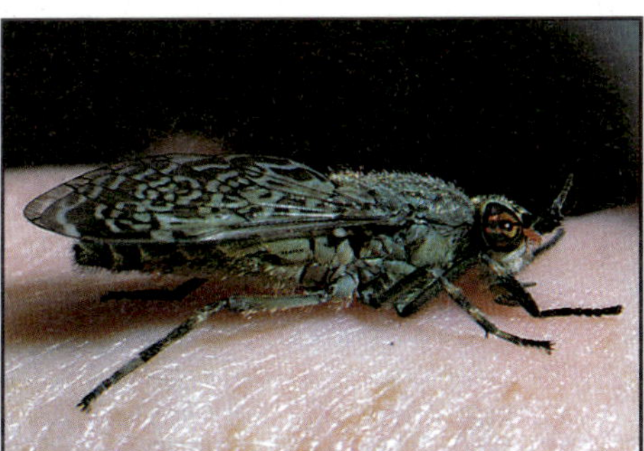

Length: 10–12 mm.
Season: May–October.
Where is it found? Throughout the British countryside.
Insect facts: The larvae live in soil which needs to be only moderately damp, which explains why this species is so widespread.

Thunder Fly

Scientific name: *Chrysops caecutiens*
Family: Tabanidae

Appearance: The striking beauty of the iridescent eyes is small comfort when one of these flies has just sunk its proboscis into your skin. This is the commonest of several similar species with black-spotted wings, and a brown abdomen patterned with black. The black pattern on this species is denser than in the very similar *Chrysops relictus* which tends to be restricted to heaths and moorland.

Length: 10 mm.

Season: May–September.

Where is it found? In most rural habitats, but usually near water, throughout the British Isles.

Large Bee Fly

Scientific name: *Bombylius major*
Family: Bombyliidae

Appearance: The body is densely clothed in long brown hairs, although these gradually wear off as the insect ages, so that old specimens are only thinly clad. The front half of each wing bears a broad black band, with a wavy rear edge. The long, slim, needle-like black proboscis (feeding tube) is held out straight in front when the insect is at rest. When feeding at flowers it maintains a semi-hover, with the front legs – and sometimes all six legs – remaining in contact with the flower.
Length: 10–12 mm (excluding the proboscis).
Season: March–May.
Where is it found? Throughout England and Wales, northwards to southern Scotland, but rare in Ireland.
Insect facts: The female 'bombs' the nest entrances of solitary bees by hovering over them and dropping her eggs inside. The bee fly larva kills the bee larva and consumes its provisions.

Robber Fly

Scientific name: *Dysmachus trigonus*
Family: Asilidae

Appearance: This is one of many similar-looking, hairy, blackish robber flies. The various species are not easy to distinguish. All robber flies are predators, and have heavily spined legs for maintaining a secure grip on struggling prey. The body is much slimmer than in most flies, and the abdomen is generally hump-shaped on top. There is usually a moustache of downward-pointing hairs on the 'face'.
Length: 14–20 mm.
Season: May–August.
Where is it found? In sandy places, especially on coastal dunes, throughout the British Isles.
Insect facts: *Philonicus albiceps* is also common on coastal dunes but has a pale-grey abdomen.

Dance Fly

Scientific name: *Empis livida*
Family: Empididae

Appearance: Dance flies can easily be recognized by the very stout black proboscis which projects downwards beneath the head. The legs are fairly long, the abdomen slim, and the thorax bulges on top, giving these insects a hump-backed stance. This species is mainly brown, with reddish eyes. Male dance flies are predators but also feed on flowers which is the females' normal habit. The males perform aerial mating dances, during which they present the female with a 'wedding gift' – a dead insect.
Length: 8–9 mm.
Season: July–August.
Where is it found? Along hedgerows and woodland rides, and in marshes, throughout the British Isles.
Insect facts: *Empis tessellata* is also very common, but is bigger (10–12 mm), much hairier, and black rather than brown.

Wing-flick Fly

Scientific name: *Poecilobothrus nobilitatus*
Family: Dolichopodidae

Appearance: The male (illustrated) is dark metallic green, tinted with red. The sides of the thorax are grey, the eyes reddish, and the head rather small. The wings are black with prominent white tips, and project well beyond the tip of the abdomen. The female is smaller, duller, and lacks the white wing-tips. The larvae are aquatic, and the adults often throng in thousands on the surface of ponds. There are numerous similar green species, but all lack the white wing-tips.

Length: Male 6 mm; female 4–5 mm.

Season: May–August.

Where is it found? By ponds and puddles, throughout the British Isles.

Insect facts: During courtship the male stands just in front of the female and rapidly flicks his wings back and forth, displaying their white tips.

Hover-fly

Scientific name: *Syrphus ribesii*
Family: Syrphidae

Appearance: This is one of many similar-looking hover-flies with yellow-and-black wasp-like stripes on the abdomen. The most common of these are probably *Syrphus ribesii* and the almost identical (but rather smaller) *Syrphus vitripennis*, together with *Metasyrphus corollae*. All three species can often be found thronging together on flowers such as Wild Angelica (*Angelica sylvestris*).
Length: 11–13 mm.
Season: June–October.
Where is it found? In every kind of habitat throughout the British Isles.
Insect facts: In all three species (and in many similar ones) the slug-like larvae feed on aphids.

Hover-fly

Scientific name: *Scaeva pyrastri*
Family: Syrphidae

Appearance: This species is usually recognized quite easily by its conspicuous black-and-white abdomen, but the white markings can sometimes be replaced by pale cream. The abdomen is longer and more parallel-sided than in *Syrphus* or *Metasyrphus*. The white, lunule-shaped markings slope upwards at their inner ends. In the similar *Scaeva selenitica*, they are arranged more or less on one level across the abdomen.
Length: 16–17 mm.
Season: May–November.
Where is it found? In most habitats, including gardens, but rare in Scotland.

Hover-fly

Scientific name: *Episyrphus balteatus*
Family: Syrphidae

Appearance: This black-and-orange species is less wasp-like than most of the other really common striped hover-flies. The top of the thorax is shiny blackish gold, marked with two longitudinal pale stripes. Note how the eyes meet on top of the head in the insect illustrated, indicating that this is a male, a feature that is common to most hover-flies. This species is a great migrant, and vast swarms often arrive via the English Channel from continental Europe.
Length: 10 mm.
Season: May–November.
Where is it found? Just about anywhere.

Hover-fly

Scientific name: *Leucozona lucorum*
Family: Syrphidae

Appearance: The eyes of this attractive hover-fly are very hairy. The thorax is a rich golden brown, the front half of the abdomen is whitish cream, and the rear half black. It bears some resemblance to a very small bumble-bee, but not to the extent of some other hover-flies, such as *Volucella bombylans*.
Length: 12 mm.
Season: May–September.
Where is it found? On flowers in woodland rides, along shady lanesides, and on shaded riverbanks, throughout the British Isles.

Snout-faced Hover Fly

Scientific name: *Rhingia campestris*
Family: Syrphidae

Appearance: The abdomen of this distinctive hover-fly is plain brown, while the thorax is bronzy black. This is one of only two hover-flies in Britain with a conspicuous long, snout-like projection on the face. The other, *Rhingia rostrata*, is so rare that it is unlikely to be seen. When *Rhingia campestris* is feeding on flowers, as in the illustration, the long proboscis is extended downwards from a flexible membrane within the snout.
Length: 11–12 mm.
Season: May–October.
Where is it found? In most kinds of habitats, throughout the British Isles.
Insect facts: The larvae live in dung, especially cow-pats.

Bumble-bee Fly

Scientific name: *Volucella bombylans*
Family: Syrphidae

Appearance: In one form of this fly (not illustrated) the front half of the thorax is black, followed by a yellow band. There is another yellow band at the front of the abdomen, followed by a broad black band, and finally a white hairy tail. This form mimics the White-tailed and Small Garden Bumble-bees, among others. A second form (illustrated) is entirely black, save for a reddish-orange tail. This form mimics the Red-tailed Bumble-bee and other similar species. Other flies that mimic bumble-bees lack the feathery hairs on the arista (the whip-like extension on the antenna, clearly visible in the illustration).

Length: 13–14 mm.
Season: May–October.
Where is it found? This is mainly a woodland-edge species, but it is also common in many other habitats, throughout the British Isles.
Insect facts: The larvae live as harmless scavengers inside bees' nests – often the very species that are mimicked by the adult fly.

Hover-fly

Scientific name: *Volucella pellucens*
Family: Syrphidae

Appearance: This large species is shiny rather than hairy. The thorax is black, with reddish-brown sides. The front half of the abdomen is mainly whitish, the rear half shiny black. The abdomen in *Leucozona lucorum* is similar, but its lovely reddish-brown, hairy thorax and much smaller size easily serve to distinguish it from *Volucella pellucens*.
Length: 12–14 mm.
Season: May–October.
Where is it found? Mainly in woodland rides, but also in the open if woodlands are close by, throughout the British Isles.
Insect facts: The larvae live as scavengers inside the nests of paper wasps.

Tapered Drone-fly

Scientific name: *Eristalis pertinax*
Family: Syrphidae

Appearance: Like the Drone-fly (*Eristalis tenax*) this species mimics the Honey Bee (*Apis mellifera*). In *Eristalis pertinax* the abdomen tapers away strongly towards the rear, and the feet (tarsi) on the front and middle legs are black. *Eristalis tenax* has a much chunkier abdomen, with scarcely any taper and a virtually flat rear end; the tarsi on the front and middle legs are yellowish.
Length: 14–16 mm.
Season: March–November, but most common August–October.
Where is it found? Just about anywhere.
Insect facts: The larvae of both species are called rat-tailed maggots. They live in water or wet manure-heaps and have a long tail-like breathing siphon.

Dwarf Drone-fly

Scientific name: *Eristalis arbustorum*
Family: Syrphidae

Appearance: This is much like a miniature version of *Eristalis tenax* or *Eristalis pertinax*, but size alone is enough of a distinction. It is more difficult to distinguish *Eristalis arbustorum* from the equally common *Eristalis nemorum*. The former has a black or brown last segment to the antenna (*see* illustration), while in the latter this last segment is orange.
Length: 9–11 mm.
Season: April–October.
Where is it found? In all habitats, throughout the British Isles.

Elegant Drone-fly

Scientific name: *Eristalis horticola*
Family: Syrphidae

Appearance: In this species the triangular markings near the front of the abdomen are larger and of a much brighter orange than in *Eristalis tenax* and *Eristalis pertinax*. In *Eristalis horticola* there is also a conspicuous yellowish-orange line between each abdominal segment. Finally, there is a cloudy patch across the middle of the wings, not found in the other species.
Length: 14–16 mm.
Season: May–October.
Where is it found? This species is less common than the others, and is mainly found in woodland rides, but it is very widespread.

Dwarf Bumble-bee Fly

Scientific name: *Eristalis intricarius*
Family: Syrphidae

Appearance: This species is like a miniature form of one of the white-tailed bumble-bees. It is also very similar to the white-tailed form of *Volucella bombylans*,

but is much smaller, and the front of the abdomen is black, not the yellow of *Volucella bombylans*. The tops of the head and thorax in *Eristalis intricarius* are also usually covered in short coats of attractive tawny hairs, though these do tend to wear off, revealing varying amounts of the black beneath.
Length: 10–12 mm.
Season: May–September.
Where is it found? Mainly on woodland edges, but also on heaths, moors, and downs.

Hover-fly

Scientific name: *Helophilus pendulus*
Family: Syrphidae

Appearance: The longitudinal stripes on top of the thorax easily distinguish this species from any wasp-like members of other genera. This is also a much chunkier-bodied fly than most of the other really common yellow-and-black species. It has a black stripe down the middle of the face, absent in other similar-looking *Helophilus* species, except for *Helophilus hybridus*. In the latter species, only the basal third of the hind tibia is yellow; in *Helophilus pendulus* this proportion is two-thirds.
Length: 10–14 mm.
Season: April–October.
Where is it found? In all kinds of habitats, throughout the British Isles, and common in gardens.
Insect facts: Although this species is most often seen on flowers, the males are often noticed hovering about 30 centimetres above the surfaces of ponds.

Bulb-fly

Scientific name: *Merodon equestris*
Family: Syrphidae

Appearance: This species mimics a whole range of different bumble-bees. The fly illustrated is one of the more common forms, but red-tailed and white-tailed varieties are also very abundant, and all occur together. The Bulb-fly is a more narrow-bodied, hunch-backed, and less plump-looking fly than *Volucella bombylans*, which has a feathery arista (the tiny whip-like extension on the antenna). The arista is bare in the Bulb-fly.
Length: 11–13 mm.
Season: April–October.
Where is it found? In most habitats, but especially in gardens, throughout the British Isles.
Insect facts: The larva lives inside bulbs and can be a pest of daffodils, irises, and other cultivated flowers.

Tawny Bumble-bee Fly

Scientific name: *Criorrhina berberina*
Family: Syrphidae

Appearance: The uniformly tawny pelt of this attractive species is unlike that of any other hover-fly; it mimics bees such as the Carder Bee (*Bombus pascuorum*). As in the Bulb-fly (*Merodon equestris*), and unlike in the Bumble-bee Fly (*Volucella bombylans*), the arista (whip-like extension) on the antenna is bare.
Length: 13–14 mm.
Season: June–August.
Where is it found? Mainly in woodland rides, but quite locally.

Hover-fly

Scientific name: *Myiatropa florea*
Family: Syrphidae

Appearance: In some ways, this species is similar to the Drone-fly, *Eristalis tenax*, but the abdomen is broader and much yellower, and the pattern on top of the thorax is very distinctive (*see* illustration). Although it is common, *Myiatropa florea* is never seen in the numbers typical of some *Eristalis* species. The larvae have been found in pools of water in decaying tree stumps.
Length: 14–16 mm.
Season: May–October.
Where is it found? Usually on flowers, throughout the British Isles, mostly in woodland rides, but not uncommonly in gardens.

Hover-fly

Scientific name: *Chrysotoxum cautum*
Family: Syrphidae

Appearance: This species, and one or two other members of the same genus, are easily the best mimics of wasps found in Britain. The mode of flight and general appearance are very wasp-like, and only an expert can tell the difference without a very close inspection. Note the unusually long antennae and the yellow-ringed scutellum (at the rear of the thorax), resembling a very broad flat U. The adults are found on flowers or perched on low vegetation. The larvae live inside ants' nests.

Length: 13 mm.
Season: May–August.
Where is it found? Mainly in woodland rides and along hedgerows, but restricted to southern and central areas of the country.

Common Wasp-fly

Scientific name: *Conops quadrifasciata*
Family: Conopidae

Appearance: The long, conspicuously clubbed antennae, broad head, and slim, club-shaped abdomen all serve to identify this fly as a member of the family Conopidae. The slim proboscis is long and straight, and cannot be folded away, but projects in front of the head when not in use. This is much the commonest of the black-and-yellow wasp-like species. *Conops flavipes* is similar, but much rarer, and can be distinguished by its black hind femora (these are yellowish in the species illustrated).
Length: 8–12 mm.
Season: June–September.
Where is it found? Mostly in woodland rides, over much of the British Isles.
Insect facts: The female lays its eggs on the backs of paper wasps, ambushing them on flowers or as they return to the nest. A male will often ride around for hours on a female's back, as illustrated.

Burdock Fruit-fly

Scientific name: *Trypeta tussilaginis*
Family: Tephritidae

Appearance: Most of the flies in this family have spotted wings and beautiful iridescent eyes, often combining two or three colours. In the female, the ovipositor is telescopic and can be extruded to its full length and forced deep into plant tissues to introduce the eggs. Some species cause conspicuous galls (swellings) on their host plants. Numerous similar-looking species occur on a wide range of plants, but especially on thistles, knapweeds, and other members of the daisy family. The species illustrated lives mainly on Lesser Burdock (*Arctium minus*). Look out for the tiny flies waving their wings as they walk around on the flower buds. Wing-waving is a typical habit seen in most members of the family Tephritidae.

Length: 7–8 mm.
Season: July–August.
Where is it found? On Burdock plants throughout much of the country.

Stilt-legged Fly

Scientific name: *Calobata cibaria*
Family: Micropezidae

Appearance: The long, stilt-like legs from which the common name is derived will be obvious from the illustration. Note also the long thin body and rather rounded head. Stilt-legged Flies are predators, but probably also behave as scavengers by taking advantage of prey discarded by other larger hunters. These flies are most often seen stalking slowly around on leaves in damp shady places. The larvae develop in decaying vegetable matter.
Length: 10 mm.
Season: May–August.
Where is it found? In damp shady woodlands and marshes.

Red-eyed Snail-fly

Scientific name: *Tetanocera assogans*
Family: Sciomyzidae

Appearance: The body colour is light brown, with greyish dusting on the sides of the thorax, and prominent reddish-orange eyes. Note the hollowed-out front to the head. Snail-fly larvae feed on slugs and snails. Some are aquatic, and kill their prey rapidly. Others live inside the shells of land snails, slowly eating the snail from the inside out.
Length: 9–10 mm.
Season: May–August.
Where is it found? In dense vegetation, usually near ponds.

Spot-winged Manure-fly

Scientific name: *Sepsis fulgens*
Family: Sepsidae

Appearance: These small, shiny black flies spend most of their time parading around on leaves or on cow-pats, busily waving their wings, each of which bears a black spot towards the tip. They may also be found in some numbers on flowers such as Wild Angelica (*Angelica sylvestris*). *Sepsis fulgens* is rather special because, in late summer, it forms huge swarms containing many thousands of flies. These all scurry around frantically waving their wings with gusto yet to no apparent purpose, and we still do not understand why these swarms are generated.
Length: 5–6 mm.
Season: April–October.
Where is it found? Mainly in woodland rides and on cow-pats in meadows, throughout the British Isles.
Insect facts: The larvae develop inside dung.

Yellow Swarming Fly

Scientific name: *Thaumatomyia notata*
Family: Chloropidae

Appearance: The thorax and abdomen are marked with black and yellow bands, but you will need a magnifying glass to see them, because this is a very small fly. What it lacks in size, however, it makes up for in numbers, and this fly often swarms in thousands in early autumn. Most swarms occur on the outside walls of buildings, but they sometimes crop up inside houses, on ceilings. The swarms seem to be formed prior to hibernation because the winter is spent in the adult state.

Length: 2 mm.
Season: All year.
Where is it found? Practically everywhere, because the larvae feed on grasses.

Parasite-fly

Scientific name: *Tachina fera*
Family: Tachinidae

Appearance: Like most parasite-flies, this species is conspicuously bristly, especially on the abdomen. The wing-bases are heavily tinged with yellowish orange, while the yellow hair on the face and broad black stripe down the middle of the abdomen distinguish this fly from similar species. *Alophora hemiptera* also has a broad black abdominal stripe, but it is a very strange, flattened fly with (in the female) heavy black clouding on the frontal part of the wings, and no bristles. *Gonia divisa* is also similar, but far smaller (9–10 mm), with a swollen head and no orange wing-bases. *Tachina grossa* is a large and very bristly black species.

Length: 10–15 mm.

Season: April–October.

Where is it found? On flowers, mainly in woodland rides, marshes, and around the edges of ponds and lakes, throughout the whole country.

Insect facts: The female lays her eggs on leaves. When the larvae hatch, they bore their way into caterpillars and feed on them from the inside.

Flesh-fly

Scientific name: *Sarcophaga carnaria*
Family: Sarcophagidae

Appearance: The large size, big feet, red eyes, and chequered black-and-silver pattern on the abdomen, are all typical features of this genus, although the individual species are not easy to distinguish. Flesh-flies are often found on flowers and rotting fruit, but they also bask in small groups on logs and large stones. The females give birth to live larvae which are dropped on to dung or small animal corpses.

Length: 12–20 mm.

Season: All year.

Where is it found? Just about anywhere.

Bluebottle and Greenbottle

Scientific name: *Calliphora vomitoria* and *Lucilia caesar*
Family: Calliphoridae

Appearance: There are two Bluebottles on the left and one Greenbottle on the right. Females of both species lay their eggs on meat, such as on the corpse of this baby bird that had fallen out of the nest. There are many species of bluebottles and greenbottles, but they cannot easily be distinguished. Any greenbottles noted on cow-pats or basking in some numbers on a farm gate will probably be two common members of the family Muscidae, *Dasyphora cyanella* (with hairy eyes) or *Orthellia cornicina* (with green jowls – silvery jowls in *Lucilia caesar*).
Length: Bluebottle 10–12 mm; Greenbottle 8–15 mm.
Season: All year.
Where are they found? Just about anywhere.

Noonday-fly

Scientific name: *Mesembrina meridiana*
Family: Muscidae

Appearance: With its shiny black body and bright-orange wing-bases, this is one of the easiest of our flies to recognize. It is often seen basking on leaves and tree trunks, but it is also fond of visiting flowers, especially brambles and umbellifers, such as Wild Angelica (*Angelica sylvestris*). It is also common on Ivy blossoms in autumn. The females are found on cow-pats where they lay their eggs.
Length: 10–12 mm.
Season: March–October.
Where is it found? In meadows, woods, and lanesides, throughout the British Isles.

Spotted Flower-fly

Scientific name: *Graphomya maculata*
Family: Muscidae

Appearance: The female (illustrated) is silvery grey, marked with black spots. In the male the abdomen is brown, with a few black markings. The eyes in both sexes are hairy. The adults are usually seen on flowers, often in large numbers on white umbels such as Hogweed (*Heracleum sphondylium*) and Wild Angelica (*Angelica sylvestris*). The carnivorous larvae dwell in the mud at the bottoms of ponds and puddles, and in rotting vegetable matter.
Length: 9–10 mm.
Season: June–October.
Where is it found? Mostly in damp woodland rides and lanesides, throughout the British Isles.

Yellow Dung-fly

Scientific name: *Scathophaga stercoraria*
Family: Scathophagidae

Appearance: The males are covered in a dense pelt of golden hairs, and are larger than the females, which are less densely hairy and tend to be greenish yellow. The antennae are black. The males gather in large numbers on cow-pats and other animal dung, grabbing any female that arrives to lay her eggs. The males are often seen far away from dung and are predators, feeding on other insects such as hover-flies and crane flies.

Length: 8–10 mm.
Season: April–October.
Where is it found? Mostly in pastures, but also in a variety of other habitats, throughout the country.
Insect facts: Several other rarer species are similar, but less golden, with red eyes and orange antennae.

Checklist and Index of Common Names

Entries or part-entries in **bold type** refer to the names under which the insects in this Michelin Field Guide are listed throughout the book. Other entries refer to other species or to alternative names that occur within the main entries.